CLOUD MIGRATION FOR EXECUTIVES

A PHASED APPROACH TO COMPLETE CLOUD READINESS

J. S. SANDHU

INDIA • SINGAPORE • MALAYSIA

ISBN 979-8-89277-612-7

Contents

Phase 6
Managing Cloud Phase

Case Studies

Cloud Migration for Executives

Cloud migration stands as a pivotal decision affecting an organization's entire IT setup and business functions. For senior management and executives strategizing the organization's direction, comprehending the significance of cloud migration is essential. Below are key reasons underscoring the importance of this transition:

Cost Efficiency:

Adopting cloud migration can lead to substantial financial benefits. The cloud's pay-for-what-you-use model ensures that organizations only spend on resources they actively use, aiding in more accurate financial forecasts and budgeting. This approach also eliminates the hefty initial costs typically associated with in-house IT infrastructure. A prominent example is Zoom's 2020 move to the cloud. This strategic decision, spurred by the pandemic-induced demand surge for video conferencing, allowed Zoom to evade considerable upfront infrastructure costs and realize major savings.

Scalability:

Cloud services excel in their adaptability, allowing businesses to adjust their IT resources based on current needs. This flexibility is particularly vital in sectors with variable demand patterns. Take the travel industry, which sees a significant increase in activity during holiday seasons. Cloud solutions enable these companies to efficiently scale their IT infrastructure to meet high seasonal demands and downscale in slower periods, optimizing costs. A case in point is Delta Airlines, which recently transitioned its data center to the cloud, enhancing both scalability and overall system performance.

Security:

Cloud platforms offer advanced security features including robust data encryption, network safeguards, and proactive threat management. This aspect is crucial for top executives responsible for protecting organizational data amidst escalating cybersecurity threats. Cloud solutions provide an additional security barrier, crucial in today's digital landscape. A notable instance is Capital One's 2020 cloud migration, aimed at bolstering security and minimizing data breach risks.

Increased Collaboration:

Cloud technology is instrumental in enhancing collaboration and supporting the current trends of remote working. This aspect is particularly vital for businesses with a workforce spread across different locations. Cloud platforms offer a centralized hub for seamless team collaboration, simplifying information sharing and joint efforts. Slack's recent transition to cloud services to bolster remote working capabilities during the pandemic serves as a prime example. This move significantly improved teamwork and communication among its worldwide employees.

Competitive Advantage:

Transitioning to the cloud can endow organizations with a distinct competitive advantage. By adopting the latest in cloud computing, businesses can stay ahead in the market race. Cloud services enable quicker innovation, rapid deployment of new offerings, and valuable insights through data analytics. Netflix's cloud migration is an exemplary case in this regard. By shifting to cloud-based solutions, Netflix significantly outpaced traditional cable TV services, leveraging the cloud's power to enhance its streaming services and market positioning.

Introduction

Cloud migration has become increasingly popular as organizations seek to modernize their IT infrastructure and take advantage of the benefits of cloud technology. However, migrating to the cloud can be a complex process that requires careful planning and execution. That's why the cloud migration process is broken down into six phases.

Phase 1: Cloud Assessment

This initial phase revolves around a comprehensive evaluation of the current IT setup to gauge the viability and potential benefits of a cloud migration. It involves a broad assessment, preparation of a server list, thorough evaluation of applications, and a readiness check for cloud migration. Crucial in this phase is the assessment of various migration strategies like replace model, retire approach, lift/shift approach, and versioning, allowing organizations to determine the most suitable path forward. This stage lays the groundwork for a seamless cloud transition.

Phase 2: Database Mapping with Applications

In this phase, the focus is on aligning databases with respective applications, closely examining data interdependencies. This step is instrumental in identifying any potential migration challenges and ensuring seamless data transfer to the cloud. Employing clustering techniques is crucial here, as it helps in organizing databases effectively for efficient management.

Phase 3: Mobilizing Phase

This phase is where the actionable cloud migration plan is crafted. Organizations select their cloud service provider through a detailed RFP process and make decisions regarding tools and services needed for the migration. This stage encompasses licensing and cost analysis, operational expense assessments, policy setting, and conducting a landing zone assessment to prepare the cloud environment for the incoming workloads.

Phase 4: Migration Phase

The migration phase is the practical execution of transferring workloads to the cloud. It encompasses various approaches like lift and shift migration, migration of simpler data and applications, and the transfer of more complex apps and databases. The focus here is on ensuring accurate migration, data security, and proper configuration of the cloud environment.

Phase 5: Cloud Operate Phase

Post-migration, the focus shifts to managing and operating the new cloud environment. This involves establishing a new operational model, setting up a support framework, forming cloud infrastructure teams, and undertaking server and instance costing analyses to maximize resource utilization.

Phase 6: Cloud Managed Services

The final phase involves the ongoing management and optimization of the cloud environment. This includes establishing a ticketing and support system, setting up cloud alert notifications, tackling infrastructure issues, adopting a hybrid team support model, and continuously improving through an optimization stage for further enhancements.

PHASE 1

CLOUD ASSESSMENT

CHAPTER 1

Macro Level Cloud Migration Assessment

In the competitive world of IT, maintaining an edge requires a thorough understanding of every aspect of your ecosystem. That's where a comprehensive macro-level cloud migration assessment comes into play. Think of it as conducting a meticulous top-to-bottom review of your IT system. Let's take the example of Zoho, the Indian software giant. When they sought to cater to their rapidly expanding global clientele and enhance their suite of SaaS applications, they recognized the need to proceed with caution and avoid blind leaps. They rolled up their sleeves and dug deep, evaluating everything from their server health to their application responsiveness. Through such a comprehensive assessment, they managed to weave a strategy that wasn't just about moving to the cloud but doing it smartly, ensuring every bit of data had its rightful place and every application ran at its peak. It's about making the cloud not just a destination, but a strategic journey tailored to an organization's heartbeat. This review looks at the complete IT picture, from servers and applications to databases and storage solutions.

Define goals and objectives:

When deciding to transition your company's IT infrastructure to the cloud, it's similar to moving homes. Before you relocate, you'd scout the new area, plan the move, and ensure your cherished belongings safely make the journey. This process, in the realm of IT, is termed a "macro level cloud migration assessment." Essentially, you're mapping out your IT belongings and determining how best to transition them to their new cloud home.

1. **Identify the problem or opportunity:** Recognize the challenges or opportunities prompting this migration. Maybe it's an aging IT system akin to a rickety old car guzzling money or perhaps a desire to streamline operations like adopting a sleek, new high-speed train. General Electric (GE) recognized the need to adapt to the digital era, addressing the challenges of an aging IT infrastructure and aiming for more efficient operations. The opportunity? Transforming into a digital-industrial company.
2. **Involve stakeholders:** Just as family members voice preferences for a holiday destination, involve IT and business folks in this process. Their collective insights paint a clearer migration picture. When Dow Jones aimed for a massive cloud migration, it wasn't just an IT decision. They involved various teams, from business to tech, ensuring everyone's needs were considered.
3. **Use the SMART framework:** Just saying, "Let's move to the cloud" is vague. It's like saying, "Let's go on vacation!" But where? For how long?. Using the SMART framework, goals

become precise, like, "Migrate 80% of applications to the cloud within a year, aiming for a 25% cost reduction." Capital One's cloud migration journey is a testament to the effectiveness of SMART goals. They aimed to not only migrate a significant portion of their operations but also enhance agility and customer experience.

4. **Ranking Priorities:** Some goals are crucial, like ensuring business-critical apps have a seamless transition. As Netflix transitioned to the cloud, prioritization was vital. They ranked their migration based on the importance of each application to their business, customer impact, and potential for cost savings.
5. **Broadcasting the Vision:** Ensure everyone's in the loop. It's about sharing the migration roadmap, so all stakeholders are on the same journey. During the US government's cloud initiatives, ensured all departments and stakeholders were in sync, utilizing channels appropriate for the organization.

Inventory current IT infrastructure:

Taking stock of your current IT assets is pivotal before considering any migration steps. This inventory provides a clear picture of the landscape and helps anticipate any challenges during the move. Here's how:

1. **Listing Possessions:** Start with listing down every piece of IT hardware, software, and data center. It's essential to capture both tangible and intangible assets, irrespective of whether they're owned or leased.
2. **Detailed Cataloging:** Dive deeper by gathering specifications of each asset. This would include details like make and model, software versions, operating system, network configurations, and IP addresses.
3. **Organizing Items:** Organize assets based on their function, location, and significance. Differentiating between servers,

storage solutions, applications, databases, and networking equipment aids in streamlined migration. Ensure each asset has a unique identifier for effortless tracking.

4. **Condition Check:** Assess the current condition of the IT assets. Gauge their compatibility with the new cloud environment and determine if upgrades or replacements are necessary.
5. **Documenting Everything:** Consolidate all this information in an organized manner, preferably in a structured database or spreadsheet. This documentation acts as a vital reference during the migration process.
6. **Double-Checking:** Validation ensures accuracy. Collaborate with the IT team and other stakeholders to reaffirm the inventory's completeness and correctness. Update where needed based on feedback.

Analyze Business and Technical Requirements:

Diving into a cloud migration without clear requirements is like setting off on a journey without a map. The journey's success is intricately tied to understanding both the business landscape and technical necessities. These requirements steer the choice of cloud model and services. Here's how to decode this complex puzzle:

1. **Engaging Stakeholders:** Spotlight every group that the migration would touch – from business users and IT brigades to diverse departments. For instance, when Capital One embarked on its cloud journey, they ensured alignment across multiple teams, avoiding siloed decision-making.
2. **Listing Business Desires:** Ask the question, "Why are we moving to the cloud?" It might be to streamline operations, cut down on expenses, or boost business agility. These requirements should mirror the grander organizational objectives.
3. **Define technical requirements:** Here, it's all about the 'hows'. How do we need the cloud to perform? How can we maintain top-notch security while ensuring scalability? When Adobe

transitioned to a cloud-based model, they placed a strong emphasis on these technical dimensions, from ensuring high performance to robust security mechanisms.

4. **Highlighting Essentials:** Prioritize what's non-negotiable. Not all requirements wear the same hat of importance. Some are critical drivers, while others are nice-to-have. Rank them considering their relevance to the core business processes and the value they bring.
5. **Gap Identification:** Now, juxtapose the current IT state with the envisioned cloud setting. This reveals any disparities that need addressing. A gap analysis is akin to what Airbnb did in its early stages, realizing their infrastructure wasn't equipped for their growth, leading them to embrace cloud solutions.
6. **Develop a requirements document:** Incorporate all these findings into a cohesive document. Think of it as a blueprint for the cloud migration journey. This document becomes the reference point, and just as with any significant project, it warrants thorough scrutiny and consensus from all involved parties.

Assess the Application Portfolio:

Navigating your current application portfolio and deciding which ones are ripe for a cloud transition can be challenging. Here's a suggested path:

1. **Identify all applications:** List down every application in the organization's arsenal, from custom solutions to standard packages. Companies like Dropbox, when starting their cloud journey, recognized the importance of this comprehensive inventory.
2. **Categorize applications:** Assign labels to these applications based on their relevance to business operations, their complexity, and how cloud-ready they are. For example, an enterprise might

choose to migrate a frequently used CRM tool ahead of others due to its significance.

3. **Evaluate application architecture:** Delve deep into the structural design of each application. Does it have a modular approach similar to how Spotify employs microservices? Such insights can offer cues on the application's cloud compatibility.
4. **Analyze application dependencies:** Map the interconnections between applications. Some apps might lean heavily on others, and understanding these relationships can guide the order and method of migration. Adobe, in its cloud transition, found immense value in understanding how its suite of applications interconnected.
5. **Assess data requirements:** Examine the data each application uses - its volume, type, and any associated security mandates. When healthcare companies shift to the cloud, they often have to pay special attention to data, considering stringent regulations like HIPAA.
6. **Determine migration approach:** Tailor your migration strategy to each application. While some might slide effortlessly to the cloud in a lift-and-shift manner, others could demand a more intricate approach. Solutions like AWS offer a toolkit tailored for varying application needs, assisting in this decision-making process.
7. **Develop a migration plan:** For every application, design a blueprint that spells out the migration timeline, the resources involved, and anticipated expenses. This roadmap should be consulted with and greenlit by all involved parties.

Determine the Migration Strategy:

Navigating the optimal migration path requires a blend of understanding the current IT environment and pinpointing precise business outcomes. Let's delve into the steps that sketch out this strategy:

1. **Assess the current IT environment:** Begin by scrutinizing the existing IT assets, spanning from the tangible hardware to the diverse software applications. Recognizing these elements can help unveil any potential roadblocks. For instance, when Toyota embarked on its cloud journey, grasping their intricate IT landscape was key.
2. **Identify business requirements:** Pin down the primary motives for the cloud transition. Whether you're aiming for financial prudence, robust performance, or operational agility, these factors will sculpt the migration trajectory. Adidas, in its move to the cloud, emphasized enhancing its digital consumer engagement.
3. **Determine the best cloud environment:** Elect a cloud scenario that resonates with both the operational demands and overarching business objectives. Deliberations about cost, expandability features, and safeguarding mechanisms are pivotal. Vendors like Oracle Cloud, AWS, or Google Cloud have unique offerings tailored for specific enterprise needs.
4. **Determine the migration approach:** For every application in the roster, select the migration technique that aligns best. This could be a simple lift-and-shift or a more intricate redesigning process. As an illustration, Spotify adopted multiple migration strategies to ensure uninterrupted service to its users.
5. **Prioritize applications and workloads:** Position applications by evaluating their significance, technical challenges, and affinity with the cloud. This assessment aids in orchestrating the sequence of migration. During its cloud transition, Airbus prioritized applications pivotal to their aerospace innovations.
6. **Develop a migration plan:** Draft a comprehensive migration blueprint for each application, encompassing timelines, manpower, and financial outlines. Securing an agreement from all stakeholders before initiating the transition is indispensable.

7. **Test and validate:** Pre-emptively simulate the migration process to detect potential pitfalls and certify that the strategy dovetails with the corporate objectives. Firms like LEGO meticulously tested their cloud setups to ensure users enjoyed a consistent, high-quality experience after the shift.

Evaluate the Cloud Providers:

Choosing the right cloud provider is instrumental to the success of your cloud journey. The spectrum of choices can be daunting, but with a structured approach, the selection can be streamlined. Here's a stepwise guide to doing so:

1. **Identify Cloud Providers:** Initiate by listing down cloud providers that align with your organization's operational and technical aspirations. There's a range of public cloud offerings like AWS, Azure, or Google Cloud, and then there are bespoke private cloud solutions. Capital One, for example, moved a significant part of its infrastructure to AWS to tap into its wide array of services.
2. **Evaluate Cloud Provider Features:** Scrutinize the diverse features and offerings of each contender. Focus on aspects like cost-effectiveness, potential performance, scalability, security provisions, and adherence to compliance norms.
3. **Evaluate Cloud Provider Support:** Gauge the quality of customer service of each provider. Factors like their availability, speed of response, and technical prowess are vital. Dropbox's shift from AWS to their own private cloud was, in part, driven by the need for tailored support and infrastructure control.
4. **Evaluate Cloud Provider Track Record:** Review the past performance, reputation, and customer feedback of the providers. Airbnb, for instance, has been vocal about their positive experience with Google Cloud's capabilities and service consistency.

5. **Evaluate Cloud Provider Pricing:** Analyze the pricing modules of each provider. Look out for any promotional offers, bulk usage discounts, or any hidden costs that might come into play.
6. **Evaluate Cloud Provider Contract Terms:** Examine the nitty-gritty of contract conditions and service level agreements (SLAs) presented by the providers. Aspects like uptime commitment, data safeguarding measures, and exit strategies are pivotal. For instance, Snapchat's commitment to Google Cloud was clarified with a detailed understanding of SLAs and financial terms.
7. **Conduct a Proof of Concept:** Before making the final choice, initiate a hands-on test run with the shortlisted provider to ensure their offerings are congruent with your IT demands. HSBC did this with multiple cloud providers before finalizing its choice, ensuring the fit was just right.
8. **Consider Multi-cloud Strategy:** Ponder over diversifying your cloud engagement by involving multiple providers. This strategy can be a safety net against potential service disruptions and can be a tool to leverage the best of different platforms. Companies like Coca-Cola have integrated multi-cloud strategies to harness the best from different providers.

Develop a Migration Plan:

A strong migration plan is the bedrock of a successful cloud transition. It acts as a guiding beacon, ensuring that every step taken is purposeful and in the right direction. Follow these steps to create an impactful migration roadmap:

1. **Define the Scope:** Start by laying out the boundaries of the migration. Decide on the applications or tasks to be moved, the migration schedule, and any potential hurdles in the path. For instance, when Spotify decided to move to Google Cloud, they began with a clear understanding of which data elements and services they wanted to migrate.

2. **Identify Dependencies:** Chart out any interconnections between the applications or tasks. Knowing which systems rely on one another can help in synchronizing the migration. Companies like Johnson & Johnson kept track of dependencies to avoid operational hiccups during migration.
3. **Determine the Migration Approach:** Decide on the most suitable migration strategy for each system, be it lift-and-shift, re-platforming, or re-architecting.
4. **Prioritize Applications or Workloads:** Rank the applications or tasks based on their importance, intricacy, and how well they align with the cloud setup. When Philips moved to the cloud, they first transitioned their most crucial and cloud-compatible systems.
5. **Define the Target Cloud Environment:** Detail out the desired cloud setup, encompassing your chosen cloud service provider, the preferred region, and the specific services you'd want to leverage.
6. **Define the Migration Plan:** Craft a comprehensive migration blueprint, detailing timelines, resources, budgets, and any tweaks needed for the applications to adapt to the new cloud environment.
7. **Define the Migration Testing Plan:** Create a strategy to test the migrated systems, ensuring that they run seamlessly in the new setup. Adobe, when shifting to the cloud, incorporated a robust testing phase to guarantee the efficiency of their applications post-migration.
8. **Define the Rollback Plan:** Establish a contingency plan to revert changes if anything goes amiss during the migration. This plan should cover aspects like restoring the original state or reverting to the former IT setup.
9. **Test and Validate:** Before diving into the full-scale migration, trial the plan to ascertain its viability and to preemptively tackle any unforeseen challenges.

10. **Execute the Migration Plan:** With the blueprint in hand, commence the migration. Stay vigilant, monitor the progress, and ensure that everything sticks to the pre-decided schedule. For instance, when Capital One undertook its migration, continuous monitoring and feedback loops were integral to its success.

Implement the Migration Plan:

The real action begins when you roll out the migration plan. Ensuring smooth implementation is paramount to achieving the desired outcomes. As you delve into this phase, keep in mind the goal: efficient, functional applications post-migration. Here are guiding steps to lead your implementation:

1. **Communicate with stakeholders:** Always keep the stakeholders in the loop. Informing all involved parties, from IT personnel and business units to the end-users, about the migration's progression, timelines, and potential changes is pivotal. When Dropbox decided to move out of AWS to its infrastructure, clear communication with both internal teams and customers was vital for a seamless transition.
2. **Allocate Cloud Resources:** Set up necessary cloud infrastructure, including storage, virtual machines, networking, and safeguarding features in the desired cloud environment.
3. **Ready Migration Instruments:** Prepare essential tools that aid in the migration process, covering everything from database transfer tools to those monitoring performance.
4. **Shift Applications & Workloads:** Proceed with the migration of tasks or applications to the identified cloud environment. It's essential to be vigilant during this process. When Airbnb migrated its main database to another location, they meticulously monitored each step to quickly spot and address any challenges.

5. **Examine Post-migration:** It's not just about moving; it's about moving right. Thoroughly test the recently migrated tasks or applications for functionality, performance, and other crucial parameters to ensure smooth operation.
6. **Refine the Cloud Setup:** Post-migration, evaluate the cloud setup and make necessary tweaks. For example, after shifting, Pinterest regularly reassessed its cloud setup to make effective adjustments, leading to cost savings and performance improvements.
7. **Educate the Users:** Prepare end-users for the new environment. Offer them adequate training and resources, ensuring they can navigate the new system with ease. When Adobe shifted its offerings to the cloud, training modules were rolled out to help users adapt to the new platform.
8. **Maintain & Refine:** Post-migration, it's not 'set and forget'. Keep a watchful eye on the system's performance and continually optimize to align with business requirements. When Capital One moved to the cloud, ongoing monitoring and tweaks were crucial to achieving optimal performance.

CHAPTER 2

Prepare You Server List

Getting a comprehensive list of servers is foundational when charting a course for cloud migration. Taking a systematic approach ensures no stone is left unturned. Let's walk through the procedure:

Spot Active Servers:

Begin by cataloging all operational servers - whether they're tangible servers, virtual entities, or other infrastructure elements housing applications.

Understanding the full breadth of active servers, especially in vast or multifaceted IT frameworks, can be intricate. To simplify, here are steps tailored for effective identification:

1. **Review documentation:** Initiate by exploring available resources like network blueprints, past server lists, and equipment logs. Often, these can shine a light on the servers in operation.
2. **Conduct a network scan:** Harness the power of network discovery tools to pinpoint all the network-linked entities, spotlighting undocumented servers. When companies like Barclays embarked on their digital transformation, tools that could map out their vast networks played a crucial role.
3. **Analyze log data:** Scour through records from network gear like switches or firewall logs. These logs can offer glimpses into active servers by revealing communication threads and traffic sources.
4. **Engage with IT Teams:** Hold discussions with IT personnel and application custodians. Their day-to-day interactions can unveil servers that might be hidden from scans or logs. During Cisco's migrations, dialogues with their IT specialists were invaluable in capturing the full server landscape.
5. **Inspect cloud environments:** If your organization taps into cloud platforms, delving into the cloud dashboard can uncover both virtual entities and native cloud tools in use.
6. **Analyze software licenses:** Peeking into software licensing can give cues about server activity. These licenses often indicate the server counts dedicated to specific tools or applications. When companies like Adobe transitioned to newer platforms, understanding software licenses was pivotal in shaping migration strategies.

Categorize the servers:

Proper organization and categorization of servers can dramatically streamline the cloud migration process. It's about clarity, precision, and preparedness. By categorizing servers, you create a clear roadmap that facilitates decision-making, optimizes resource allocation, and ensures each component transitions smoothly. In 2017, for instance, State Bank of India (SBI) underwent a major digital transformation. Part of this initiative was a cloud migration, where a systematic approach to server categorization became pivotal. They needed to handle vast amounts of customer data and transactions with minimal disruption. With well-defined categories, they could prioritize mission-critical servers, manage interdependencies, and plan migrations in phases. Drawing from such real-world scenarios, this chapter will guide you through effective techniques and best practices for server categorization, setting the stage for a successful migration.

Group by Function:

Servers can be organized based on their roles, such as web servers, database hosts, or application servers.

1. **Criticality:** Identify servers vital to your business operations. Such servers, like the ones handling payment gateways for e-commerce giants like Amazon, are pivotal for business continuity and often take precedence during migration.
2. **Level of Intricacy:** Group servers based on how intricate their configurations are. Those with multiple layers may demand a more comprehensive migration plan.
3. **Demand on Resources:** Assess servers by their consumption patterns of CPU, memory, and storage. High-demand servers, similar to those streaming platforms like YouTube might employ, might necessitate added cloud capacity and fine-tuning to leverage cloud capabilities.
4. **Security requirements:** Distinguish servers by their security demands, factoring in compliance needs or data sensitivity. Financial institutions like J.P. Morgan would have servers with strict security protocols, making their cloud transition demanding in terms of security configurations.
5. **Sync with Cloud:** Group servers by how easily they can mesh with cloud setups. Some might smoothly transition, while others, possibly due to proprietary technologies, might need adjustments or even a complete overhaul before cloud integration.

6. **Technological Timeline:** Some servers, owing to their age or outdated tech components, may pose challenges during migration. When Adobe shifted its services online, the transformation of older, legacy systems was a significant undertaking.
7. **Interdependencies:** Servers don't exist in isolation. Recognize those with links or dependencies on others. When a company like Salesforce, with its myriad integrated services, plans migrations, understanding these interlinked systems is paramount to ensure uninterrupted service post-migration.

Workload Analysis for Cloud Migration:

Evaluating the demands of your workloads is vital when considering cloud migration. It ensures the move to the cloud is efficient and tailored to your specific needs. Let's break down the steps involved:

1. **Identify the workload:** Identify the specific application or system set for migration. For instance, when Dropbox decided to move a significant portion of their infrastructure to the cloud, they precisely determined which components would benefit the most from this move.
2. **Understand the workload:** Understand the intricacies of its architecture. Airbnb, during its scaling phase, analyzed the structure of its reservation and recommendation systems to ensure they could efficiently operate and scale in the cloud.
3. **Determine Cloud Compatibility:** Examine how ready your workload is for the cloud. Older systems may need updates or changes. Slack, in its early days, had to optimize various parts of its system to be cloud-ready, ensuring seamless service for its users.
4. **Financial Analysis:** Study the economic implications. Look at the current resource consumption of your workload and juxtapose it with anticipated cloud expenses. Snap Inc. analyzed costs extensively when they diversified their cloud infrastructure to ensure optimal financial and operational benefits.

5. **Choose the right cloud service:** Pair your workload with the ideal cloud service. Find the best cloud service fit for the workload. For instance, a mobile application backend might best fit a Platform as a Service (PaaS) model, whereas a legacy CRM system might be suited for Infrastructure as a Service (IaaS). When Snapchat wanted scalability for its growing user base, Google Cloud's PaaS became its choice due to its ability to dynamically manage varied workloads.
6. **Plan the migration:** Draft a migration strategy. This includes marking key dates, detailing resource allocation, and strategizing on testing methods. Pinterest, during its rapid growth phase, chalked out meticulous plans for migrating and scaling various parts of its service on the cloud.

By following such a systematic approach, businesses can ensure a seamless transition to the cloud, maximizing benefits while minimizing potential pitfalls.

Analyze the dependencies:

Determine the interdependencies between the servers and their associated applications and services. This will help you to determine the order in which the servers should be migrated.

Analyzing the dependencies for cloud migration involves identifying the various components and systems that an application or workload relies on to function properly. This is crucial as dependencies can affect the performance, availability, and security of the application or workload in the cloud environment. Here are some steps that can help in the dependency analysis process:

1. **Identify the components:** Recognize all the components that the application or workload relies on, such as hardware, software, and middleware. This could include servers, databases, application servers, load balancers, and other components. For instance, when Lego started their digital journey, they dissected

their systems to identify integral components ranging from e-commerce platforms to design systems.

2. **Determine the communication patterns:** Analyze how these components interact with each other. This can be about assessing network traffic, data flows, and APIs used for communication. A relevant example can be seen with Siemens, which, during their cloud migration, had to deeply understand interactions between their diverse technologies, like their digital twin models.
3. **Evaluate the dependencies:** Delve into how these components are connected. Understand which are vital for the application's functionality, which are redundant, and which might be obsolete.
4. **Assess the compatibility:** Review how these components will fit into the cloud environment. Check if they are in line with cloud-native services and what modifications might be required.
5. **Plan the migration:** With all the data in hand, map out the migration process. This would encompass crafting a timeline, detailing resource requirements, and setting up testing and validation strategies.

Evaluate the network topology:

Consider the structure of the network and the available bandwidth for transferring data between servers.

Understanding the network topology is vital for a successful cloud migration. It ensures that the network infrastructure aligns well with the cloud, mitigating potential challenges. Below are steps to guide through this evaluation process:

1. **Identify the network components:** Recognize the integral pieces of your network setup that play a role in supporting your application or workload. This could include devices like routers, switches, firewalls, load balancers, and VPNs.

2. **Determine the network traffic:** Study the patterns and quantities of network traffic related to your application. Such insights can highlight potential network challenges.
3. **Analyze the network architecture:** Delve deep into both the physical and logical relationships between network elements. This not only uncovers potential points of failure but also potential security risks.
4. **Assess the network capacity:** Examine if the current network can manage the demands of the application in a cloud setting. Understanding bandwidth and capacity can preempt performance challenges.
5. **Evaluate the network security:** Review the security needs of your application, considering factors like compliance standards and data protection. Mastercard, given the nature of financial data it handles, invested heavily in revalidating its network security measures as it embraced cloud solutions, ensuring every transaction remained secure.
6. **Plan the network migration:** Once equipped with the above insights, chart out the process for moving network elements to the cloud. This should include a detailed timeline, resource allocation, and strategies for testing. A glimpse into Philips reveals that when transitioning their healthcare platforms to the cloud, they crafted a robust strategy, ensuring uninterrupted services for healthcare providers and patients alike.

Determine the target environment:

Pinpoint the cloud provider and the exact cloud services intended for migration.

Selecting the right target environment is crucial in cloud migration. It helps in choosing the optimal cloud platform tailored to the needs of the application. Here's a guided approach to make this decision:

1. **Examine the application or workload:** Dive into the application, evaluating its resource demands, performance

metrics, and scalability features. For instance, when Dropbox decided to transition out of Amazon's cloud in 2016, they specifically engineered a new platform named "Magic Pocket". This infrastructure was designed to handle exabytes of data, optimizing storage, retrieval times, and ensuring redundancy by leveraging customized sharding techniques.

2. **Identify the cloud service models:** Understand the nuances of different cloud service models: IaaS, PaaS, and SaaS. This knowledge aids in determining the model that's most congruent with the application's structural needs. When Slack was scaling, they notably made use of Heroku, a PaaS solution, to manage real-time data delivery using the WebSockets protocol, ensuring instantaneous message delivery for millions of users.
3. **Evaluate the cloud providers:** Thoroughly vet potential cloud providers, aligning their offerings with your specific needs. To illustrate, Airbnb during its initial scaling phase, leaned heavily on Amazon RDS (a relational database service) to manage their database operations. This helped them handle millions of new listings without a significant overhead in database management.
4. **Assess the compliance requirements:** Ensure clarity on regulatory frameworks that the application has to adhere to. For instance, Medtronic, a global leader in medical technology had to employ Azure's BAA (Business Associate Agreement) compliant services, making certain that they adhered to the strict data handling and security measures dictated by HIPAA for their patient and clinical data.
5. **Plan for migration and management:** After collecting all necessary data, design a migration roadmap. Snap Inc., for example, didn't just randomly choose Google Cloud. They specifically leveraged Google Cloud's storage and computing services, like Bigtable and Datastore, to handle the vast amounts of data generated by Snapchat stories and messages daily, ensuring robustness and minimal latency.

Create a migration plan:

Utilize the data from prior assessments to formulate a comprehensive plan detailing the sequence of server migrations, projected timelines, and necessary resources.

Crafting a migration strategy is a vital phase of the cloud migration journey, ensuring a smooth transition and operational continuity in the new cloud setup. Follow these directives to design an effective migration blueprint:

1. **Identify the scope of the migration:** Delineate which applications or workloads are slated for migration and chalk out the sequence and projected timeline. For instance, Twitter, when upgrading their architecture, transitioned from Ruby on Rails to JVM, executing a phased migration to ensure continuous service.
2. **Decide on migration methodology:** Select an approach most compatible with the application's nature, whether it's lift-and-shift, replatforming, re-architecting, or a hybrid approach. When Guardian News & Media shifted to the cloud, they employed a replatforming strategy, taking the opportunity to transition from a monolithic system to microservices.
3. **Determine the target environment:** Identify the apt cloud provider or platform tailored to the workload's resource, performance, scalability, and regulatory needs.
4. **Evaluate the dependencies:** Review interdependencies of the application with other systems. In the case of Shopify, their migration required a meticulous understanding of dependencies as they use over 100 tools and services integrated with their main Rails application.
5. **Plan for testing and validation:** Schedule testing phases post-migration, ensuring that the moved workload aligns with performance and security benchmarks. After migrating, Etsy

executed extensive performance testing, particularly focusing on their search infrastructure to maintain responsiveness.

6. **Chart out the migration flow:** Establish a detailed calendar outlining each step's specific dates - from initial planning, migration execution, to subsequent evaluations.
7. **Assign responsibilities:** Distribute tasks for every migration stage, keeping all involved parties informed of their duties. When Samsung migrated their SmartThings platform, they created specialized teams to handle discrete parts of the migration, ensuring expertise was applied at each stage.
8. **Develop a contingency plan:** Design a fallback plan to tackle unforeseen migration challenges. Nokia, during one of its migrations, kept backup infrastructure in place to switch back, ensuring zero downtime during hiccups.
9. **Develop a post-migration plan:** Craft an enduring plan for the continuous management and refinement of the newly migrated application, emphasizing regular monitoring and potential optimizations.

Test the migration plan:

Before moving forward with the live migration, it's pivotal to validate your plan in a controlled setting. Doing so can provide insights into its viability and uncover potential issues.

Proper testing is a cornerstone in the cloud migration journey. Here's how you can ensure the effectiveness of your migration plan:

1. **Formulate testing scenarios:** Draft scenarios that encapsulate every stage of the migration process. For instance, when Pinterest shifted from multiple cloud providers to a more unified approach, they designed simulations covering various data workflows to ensure no data loss or bottlenecks occurred.
2. **Define success criteria:** Determine tangible success metrics for each test, such as data consistency, uptime, and response time.

3. **Conduct a dry run:** Perform a trial migration in an environment that closely mimics the actual production setting. Twitter, during its massive data scaling needs, orchestrated controlled migrations, ensuring that real-time tweet delivery wasn't affected during the move.
4. **Analyze test results:** Meticulously analyze the outcomes from your test migrations, noting any anomalies or areas for improvement.
5. **Refine the migration plan:** Based on the insights gained, refine your strategy, which may mean adjusting timelines, resource allocations, or even the selected cloud service.
6. **Perform a conclusive test:** Execute a final test in a setting that mirrors the live environment to ensure all potential kinks have been ironed out.

CHAPTER 3

Application Assessment

Understanding your applications thoroughly is imperative before initiating cloud migration. Application assessment offers a detailed examination of your software to gauge its readiness and compatibility for a cloud transition. The main aim here is to unearth any potential challenges that might crop up during migration and strategize accordingly.

Here's how to effectively undertake application assessment for cloud transition:

Identify the Applications:

Start by cataloging all applications in operation within your enterprise. This list should encompass internally developed software and externally procured ones.

To single out the applications ripe for cloud migration, inspect the company's IT landscape and pinpoint those fitting for the transition. Here's how:

1. **Analyze the application portfolio:** Analyze your company's suite of applications to highlight those apt for cloud transition. Parameters like an application's magnitude, intricacy, and its significance in day-to-day operations can be indicators. General Electric (GE) sifted through thousands of apps, deciding which ones would migrate to the cloud and which ones would be decommissioned based on various parameters including age and utility.
2. **Determine the business value:** Measure the business relevance of every application. Gauge its harmony with the company's broader objectives and its prospective effect on daily operations.
3. **Evaluate the technical feasibility:** Study the technical aspects of shifting each application to the cloud. This includes checking its harmony with the intended cloud model and any tweaks that might be mandatory.
4. **Weigh Financial Implications:** Analyze the financial dynamics of transferring each software to the cloud. Look into potential financial advantages, operational agility enhancements, and scalability perks.
5. **Evaluate the compliance requirements:** Review any regulatory mandates associated with every application. This could be data safeguarding rules or sector-centric regulations. It's crucial to ensure the cloud model you're leaning towards complies with these.
6. **Draft a Migration Strategy:** Formulate a detailed migration plan, specifying the software chosen for migration, the methodology for each, and an associated timeline.

Evaluate the Applications

Prior to initiating the cloud migration process, a thorough review of your applications is essential. This guarantees a deep understanding of every application's characteristics, spanning its foundational architecture, adaptability, security measures, and associated compliance requirements.

Here's a systematic approach to assessing applications for cloud transition:

Identify the Applications:

Start by listing out the software products to be evaluated for cloud migration. Knowing what you're working with is the foundation for everything that follows.

1. **Examine the Application Design:** Study the application's structural design. Ascertain the demands it places on resources, its performance benchmarks, and its scalability potential. This would involve metrics like CPU usage, memory demand, network bandwidth usage, and storage needs.
2. **Test Cloud Adaptability:** Determine how ready the application is for a cloud environment. This includes identifying any changes that might be needed, its compatibility with cloud-native services, and deciding on the apt cloud service category, whether IaaS, PaaS, or SaaS.
3. **Assess the performance requirements:** Pinpoint the exact performance requirements of the software – parameters like response time, uptime, and reliability. This is pivotal to ensure that the application will function optimally post-migration.
4. **Evaluate the security requirements:** Review the security measures the application demands, taking into account regulatory compliance and the nature of its data. This step is crucial as it aids in identifying possible security loopholes and formulating a protective strategy suitable for the cloud.

5. **Map Out the Migration:** Formulate a plan for the application's transfer and its subsequent management in the chosen cloud framework. This planning phase should encompass the timeline for migration, resource allocation, and strategies for regular supervision and management.

Determine the Cloud Readiness of the Applications

Before initiating cloud migration, it's essential to gauge how well-suited each application is for a cloud-based environment. Understanding whether an application is already designed for the cloud or needs certain tweaks is critical for a smooth transition.

Here's a systematic approach to judge the cloud readiness of applications:

1. **Catalog the Applications:** Compile a list of all the software products that will be assessed for their compatibility with cloud platforms.
2. **Analyze the application architecture:** Review the intrinsic design of the application to discern its demands in terms of resources, efficiency, and scalability. For instance, an application might have been designed to function optimally with specific CPU usage, or it might have certain memory or bandwidth prerequisites.
3. **Check for Cloud Compatibility:** Determine how seamlessly the application can transition to the cloud. This entails spotting potential changes, gauging its suitability for cloud-native features, and selecting the best-fit cloud service type, be it IaaS, PaaS, or SaaS.
4. **Assess the performance requirements:** Understand the operational performance levels the software should achieve. Key indicators would include factors like timely response, continuous availability, and dependable reliability.
5. **Evaluate the security requirements:** Deep dive into the application's security specifications. This includes understanding its compliance mandates and the nature of its data. For instance,

applications dealing with financial data might have stringent regulatory requirements.

6. **Evaluate the scalability:** Analyze how well the application can adapt to changes in demand. Some applications might be able to expand their operations (scale out) while others might need to enhance their existing capacities (scale up) within the cloud.
7. **Assess the cost-benefit:** Understand the financial implications of the transition. How would moving to the cloud impact costs, operational agility, and scalability? For example, migrating a legacy system might initially seem costly, but the long-term benefits in terms of flexibility and scalability can outweigh the initial expenditure.
8. **Plan for migration and management:** Design a clear migration strategy and post-migration management plan. This encompasses setting a migration schedule, determining necessary resources, and strategizing for future oversight and management.

Determine the Best Cloud Deployment Model

Selecting the optimal cloud deployment model is essential for ensuring the efficiency, security, and cost-effectiveness of your applications in a cloud environment. The choice largely hinges on factors like the amount of customization desired, the extent of control needed, and resource consumption.

To find the right fit, consider the unique needs of your organization and applications, while also weighing the pros and cons of each model. Here's a guided approach to assist you in this process:

1. **Evaluate the public cloud:** Examine the suitability of the public cloud. Known for its broad scalability, cost savings, and user-friendly interface, the public cloud often works well for applications without stringent data privacy demands. For instance, a basic e-commerce website without country-specific data privacy rules might find the public cloud apt.

2. **Explore Private Cloud Options:** Look into the private cloud's offerings. With enhanced security and granular control, it's particularly apt for applications that prioritize data protection. Banks, given their need to safeguard sensitive financial data, often lean towards private cloud solutions.
3. **Understand the Hybrid Cloud Dynamics:** Assess the merits of the hybrid cloud, which offers a blend of public and private cloud features. It's ideal for applications with diverse needs. For example, a healthcare provider might store patient records in a private cloud due to privacy concerns but utilize the public cloud for its patient portal.
4. **Determine the compliance requirements:** Identify regulatory demands pertinent to your organization and applications. For instance, an app catering to the EU market would need to consider GDPR guidelines. Ensuring the cloud model aligns with these regulations is crucial.
5. **Evaluate the cost-benefit:** Explore the financial aspects of each model. Consider factors such as cost reductions, flexibility enhancements, and scaling capabilities. A startup, looking for quick scalability without hefty upfront costs, might find a public cloud more financially viable.
6. **Plan for migration and management:** Craft a detailed plan for moving the applications to the selected cloud model and managing them subsequently. This entails setting migration dates, listing necessary resources, and establishing a long-term oversight framework.

Identify Any Dependencies:

It's essential to recognize the interdependencies applications might have on other systems, services, or components. Such awareness paves the way for smooth cloud transitions, minimizing the risk of unforeseen challenges or overlooked requirements. Below are structured steps to guide this identification process:

1. **Identify the components:** Detail out every component playing a role in sustaining the application. This spans from servers and databases to networking tools. For instance, a CRM system might rely on a specific SQL database and communicate with an email marketing tool.
2. **Analyze the dependencies:** Draw connections between these components to understand how they interact. This exploration can reveal the foundational elements pivotal for the application's performance. E.g., an e-commerce site might be tightly linked to an inventory management system, and a disruption in one can directly affect the other.
3. **Assess the impact of migration:** Examine the effects of transitioning each piece to the cloud. This might mean tweaking configurations or even revamping certain components to suit cloud dynamics. For example, an old legacy system might need a major overhaul or a replacement to fit into a modern cloud architecture.
4. **Determine the migration order:** Plan the order of migration. This should respect the intricate web of dependencies, ensuring foundational or heavily-reliant components move first. For instance, when migrating an ERP system, you might prioritize core databases before ancillary reporting tools.
5. **Develop a migration plan:** Formulate a detailed plan that outlines the steps for migrating each component. This would include necessary changes, timelines, resource allocations, and verification methods. If a company is transitioning its HR system, the migration strategy might involve moving employee data first, followed by payroll details, while constantly verifying data integrity.
6. **Communicate with stakeholders:** Involve every individual or team with a stake in the process. Their insights can be invaluable in identifying overlooked dependencies or suggesting smoother pathways. This could mean looping in the finance department

when transitioning an invoicing system or seeking input from sales teams for a lead tracking tool's migration.

Develop a Migration Plan

When moving to the cloud, the journey is as crucial as the destination. A well-laid migration plan is like the compass guiding this journey. Reliance Jio, one of India's telecom giants, stands as a testament to this. As they expanded their digital footprint, they didn't just jump in. They had a strategy, a plan that meticulously guided their transition, ensuring consistent services for millions without a hiccup. Taking cues from such success stories, let's focus much deeper into how you can create your own migration plan with precision and foresight.

1. **Identify the scope of the migration:** Detail out which applications or workloads will make the transition. Pinpoint the sequence and timeframe of this move. For instance, a business might prioritize moving its e-commerce platform before its internal communication tools.
2. **Choose the migration approach:** Opt for a strategy that aligns with your application's needs. This could be a straightforward lift-and-shift, a more intricate replatforming, or a complete re-architecting. An online forum, for example, may benefit from replatforming to ensure it's optimized for the cloud.
3. **Determine the target environment:** Choose a cloud provider or platform tailored to the application's demands, spanning resources, performance, scalability, and regulatory needs. A healthcare application with patient data, for instance, might gravitate towards providers known for stringent data protection standards.
4. **Evaluate the dependencies:** Understand the interplay between your chosen application and other systems. Forge a strategy to seamlessly transition these intertwined components. If an accounting software interacts with a specific banking API, ensuring this link remains intact is essential.

5. **Plan for testing and validation:** Detail out how you'll test and validate the migrated elements, confirming their optimal operation, performance, and security post-migration. For instance, after migrating a booking system, one would verify real-time availability syncing and payment gateway integrations.
6. **Set a Migration Timeline:** Craft a detailed schedule, spotlighting crucial milestones like preparatory phases, the core migration, and subsequent validations. A content streaming service might set specific dates for migrating its video library, followed by user data.
7. **Assign responsibilities:** Clearly demarcate roles across every migration phase. Ensure clarity so that every participant, from tech teams to management, knows their part.
8. **Develop a contingency plan:** Anticipate potential roadblocks, from unforeseen delays to technical glitches. Having backup plans can be a lifeline in such scenarios, like having a rollback strategy if a new cloud database faces issues.
9. **Develop a post-migration plan:** Think beyond the migration. Outline how you'll continually manage, monitor, and refine the newly migrated components. For a SaaS product, this might mean regular performance audits or user feedback loops.
10. **Communicate with stakeholders:** Maintain open channels with everyone involved or affected by the migration. Their insights, from IT professionals to business leaders and regular users, can be invaluable. For example, briefing a sales team about potential downtimes can help them manage customer expectations better.

CHAPTER 4

Migration Readiness Assessment

Evaluating an organization's readiness for cloud migration involves a thorough examination of its existing IT framework. This includes assessing infrastructure components, applications, and day-to-day operational procedures to determine their compatibility with cloud environments. The goal is to identify any potential challenges or concerns that might arise during the migration and to formulate plans to address or mitigate them. Here's a breakdown of this assessment:

Identify the current state of the IT infrastructure:

Understanding the present IT setup is foundational to ensuring a seamless cloud transition. By grasping the intricacies of your current operations, you can better gauge migration feasibility and demands. Steps in this direction include:

1. **Identify the existing infrastructure components:** Spot all elements, be it servers, storage mechanisms, networking equipment, or applications. For instance, taking stock of your

physical servers might involve cataloging brands, models, and capacities.

2. **Evaluate the existing infrastructure:** Evaluate the performance, accessibility, and security status of the present setup. For example, a data center's uptime history and redundancy measures would offer insights into its reliability.
3. **Identify any technical debt:** Highlight aspects like aging hardware or legacy systems that might hinder migration. An old operating system, for instance, might not be directly supported on some cloud platforms.
4. **Assess the dependencies:** Understand how different infrastructure elements interact and rely on each other, ensuring no critical component is overlooked during migration.
5. **Analyze the workload characteristics:** Delve into aspects like storage usage patterns, peak traffic times, and required bandwidth. For instance, an e-commerce site might experience traffic spikes during sale seasons, affecting its resource needs.
6. **Evaluate the compliance requirements:** Identify if there are specific regulatory demands like GDPR for European customers or HIPAA for healthcare data in the U.S.
7. **Identify any gaps:** Spot mismatches between your current infrastructure and what's needed for a cloud transition, be it in terms of compatibility, security, or other facets.
8. **Develop a remediation plan:** Construct an action plan to rectify and resolve any identified shortfalls or challenges.

Evaluate the existing applications:

Understanding the intricacies of your applications is pivotal for a smooth transition to the cloud. Steps in this direction include:

1. **Identify the applications:** Detail out every application that's on the migration radar.
2. **Analyze the application architecture:** Understand the resource demands, performance benchmarks, and architectural nuances

of each application. For example, a real-time analytics tool might have intensive CPU and RAM needs.

3. **Check Cloud Compatibility:** Determine if applications can seamlessly migrate or if tweaks are needed. Understanding if a legacy CRM tool can move to a Platform-as-a-Service (PaaS) can guide migration strategies.
4. **Assess the performance requirements:** Ensure that applications can maintain or improve on their response times, uptime, and overall reliability post-migration.
5. **Evaluate the security requirements:** Determine the safety measures needed, especially for sensitive data or where compliance is a must. If an application handles credit card transactions, PCI DSS compliance would be crucial.
6. **Evaluate the scalability:** Estimate how applications might need to scale in response to demand surges or organizational growth. A start-up's mobile app, anticipating user growth, would prioritize scalability.
7. **Assess the cost-benefit:** Look at both the cost savings and potential benefits of the move. Transitioning a heavy-traffic website to a cloud might bring down hosting costs due to flexible scaling.
8. **Plan for migration and management:** Plan the transition and post-migration management, ensuring applications continue to function optimally in their new environments.

Network Topology Assessment

Understanding the layout and capabilities of your network is vital in ensuring a seamless migration to the cloud. Here's a methodical approach to get a grip on your network readiness:

1. **Identify the network components:** Enumerate all network-related devices, including routers, switches, firewalls, and load balancers. For example, note the specifications of a Cisco Catalyst 3850 switch or the configurations of a Juniper SRX firewall in use.

2. **Analyze the network architecture:** Understand how the network is set up regarding bandwidth usage, traffic flows, and essential security setups. Consider monitoring tools like Wireshark to get a sense of typical traffic patterns.
3. **Evaluate the network security:** Scrutinize the security mechanisms, such as firewall configurations, VPN tunnels, and Intrusion Prevention Systems. For example, inspect if there are open ports that aren't necessary for business functions.
4. **Assess the network performance:** Examine parameters like latency, packet drop rates, and jitter to confirm the network's health. Tools like Ping or Traceroute can provide insights here.
5. **Identify any network dependencies:** Identify dependencies between apps and other infrastructure elements, such as how an application interacts with a specific database on the backend.
6. **valuate the compliance requirements:** Determine if there are specific guidelines to follow, like how GDPR affects data transfer across borders.
7. **Identify any gaps:** Spot differences between your current network setup and what's needed post-migration. This could involve recognizing that the existing VPN might not suffice for increased cloud traffic.
8. **Develop a remediation plan:** Formulate a plan to address any shortcomings or challenges unearthed during the assessment.

Evaluate the organization's data security and compliance requirements:

Assessing an organization's data security and adherence to compliance standards is a pivotal aspect of preparing for migration. This ensures that sensitive data remains safeguarded and that regulatory mandates are consistently upheld both during the migration process and thereafter. The following are key steps to aid in understanding and meeting an organization's security and compliance needs:

1. **Identify the data:** Categorize the data, highlighting crucial segments like financial records or PII like customer names and addresses.
2. **Analyze the compliance requirements:** Understand all legal and industry-specific rules applicable. For instance, a healthcare entity in the U.S. would be subject to HIPAA regulations.
3. **Evaluate the data security:** Evaluate measures such as data encryption levels, access management policies, and how authentication is managed. For instance, ascertain if multi-factor authentication is in place for critical systems.
4. **Assess the impact of migration:** Contemplate on any new vulnerabilities or challenges migration might introduce. For example, transferring data might expose it to risks if not encrypted during transit.
5. **Determine the data residency requirements:** Know where data needs to reside post-migration, especially in light of regulations like data sovereignty rules in countries like Russia, which mandate specific data types to be stored within national borders.
6. **Evaluate the disaster recovery and business continuity plans:** Review your disaster recovery plans and business continuity strategies. For example, consider how backups are currently stored and if they need to be accessible from the cloud.
7. **Identify any gaps:** Detect any discrepancies between your current data protocols and post-migration needs, perhaps seeing that existing encryption might not meet cloud provider standards.
8. **Develop a remediation plan:** Devise actionable plans to bridge any identified gaps or challenges during the assessment.

Identify the business objectives and requirements for the cloud migration:

Grasping the organization's overarching goals and specific needs for cloud migration is crucial. Whether it's about cost reduction, boosting operational flexibility, or elevating the customer experience, getting clear on these objectives is essential. It ensures that the cloud migration is in sync with the broader business strategy and delivers the desired outcomes. Here's a guide to pinpointing and articulating these business objectives and requirements for your cloud migration journey:

1. **Identify the business objectives:** List down the organization's strategic intentions like cost-cutting, flexibility improvements, scaling efficiently, or boosting security. For instance, a startup might prioritize scalability to handle potential spikes in user demand.
2. **Determine the business requirements:** Understand the specifics of what needs migrating - maybe it's a legacy CRM system or certain high-traffic websites. Know the expected performance levels, uptime necessities, and financial considerations.
3. **Evaluate the impact on business operations:** Anticipate how moving to the cloud might change day-to-day operations. For instance, adopting SaaS applications may streamline workflows but require new training.
4. **Determine the return on investment (ROI):** Forecast the monetary gains, whether through operational savings or new revenue streams. For example, by transitioning to an Infrastructure as a Service (IaaS) model, a company might save on hardware maintenance costs.
5. **Identify any risks or concerns:** Spot potential hiccups, from security concerns (e.g., possible vulnerabilities in a cloud-based storage solution) to worries about becoming too dependent on a single cloud service provider.
6. **Engage with stakeholders:** Collaborate with diverse teams – from IT professionals to department heads – to gather inputs and address concerns, ensuring a collective decision-making process.
7. **Develop a migration strategy:** Based on the identified objectives and requirements, design a cloud migration blueprint

that harmonizes with business aspirations while ensuring minimal disruptions.

Determine the best cloud deployment model:

Choosing the right environment for your cloud migration is vital to cater to your organization's unique needs. Here's how you can make that pivotal choice:

1. **Evaluate the organization's requirements:** Understand the specifics of the migration, whether it involves key software suites, niche business applications, or large datasets, while considering performance, uptime, and budgetary aspects.
2. **Understand the different cloud deployment models:** Get acquainted with the various cloud configurations available, from the ubiquitous public cloud offerings to bespoke private cloud setups and the combinations in between.
3. **Evaluate the benefits and drawbacks:** For each model, list out the advantages and challenges. For instance, public clouds like AWS might offer vast scalability but might not provide the same level of customization as a dedicated private cloud.
4. **Determine the data residency requirements:** Grasp where your data can and cannot reside. Regulations in certain regions, such as the European Union's GDPR, might necessitate specific data storage protocols.
5. **Assess the existing IT infrastructure:** Inspect the existing technology infrastructure and identify how compatible it is with each cloud model. For example, some legacy systems might not be immediately suitable for a public cloud without modifications.
6. **Identify any integration challenges:** Detect issues that might arise when integrating with certain cloud environments. This could be in terms of software incompatibilities or proprietary technologies.

7. **Collaborate with Stakeholders:** Engage with various teams and individuals to make an informed decision, ensuring everyone's requirements are considered.
8. **Develop a deployment strategy:** With all the information in hand, devise a strategy that matches your organization's unique needs, focusing on achieving the best performance, reliability, security, and financial outcomes.

Develop a migration plan:

Preparing a migration plan is pivotal for a hassle-free transition to the cloud. Such a plan not only aids in a seamless transfer but also reduces chances of hiccups that might affect business continuity. Here's a guide on crafting this crucial strategy:

1. **Identify the scope of the migration:** List down the systems, applications, or workloads that are part of this migration. For example, a company might decide to first move its e-commerce platform to the cloud while leaving the accounting system for a later phase.
2. **Decide on the Migration Method:** Pick the migration strategy that's right for each component – whether it's a direct lift-and-shift, modifying the platform (replatforming), reshaping the application (re-architecting), or a mix-and-match hybrid approach.
3. **Determine the target environment:** Choose the cloud service or vendor that aligns with the technical and compliance requirements of your workloads. For instance, a health service might opt for a provider well-versed in HIPAA regulations.
4. **Evaluate the dependencies:** Recognize how your migrating system interacts with other components. If your CRM system integrates with an email marketing tool, it's crucial to ensure that this connection remains intact post-migration.
5. **Plan for testing and validation:** Plan a rigorous testing phase to ensure the moved component functions as expected,

maintaining its performance and security standards. For example, after migrating a web application, load testing can help ensure it handles peak user traffic.

6. **Develop a migration timeline:** Create a detailed calendar plotting out each migration step. This might entail initial assessments, the migration of specific components, and subsequent verification processes.
7. **Delegate Tasks:** Distribute duties amongst your team, ensuring clarity in roles. This could mean assigning database migration to one specialist while another focuses on application-level changes.
8. **Develop a contingency plan:** Prepare for unforeseen challenges. If migrating a large database takes longer than expected, having a backup plan ensures business functions continue running smoothly.
9. **Develop a post-migration plan:** Consider tasks after the initial move. This involves continuous monitoring, performance tuning, and possibly further cloud optimizations.
10. **Communicate with stakeholders:** Maintain open channels with everyone impacted, be it the IT team, department heads, or daily computer users. A weekly update, for instance, can keep teams informed about progress and potential changes in daily operations.

CHAPTER 5

Different Migration Models and Techniques for Cloud Migration

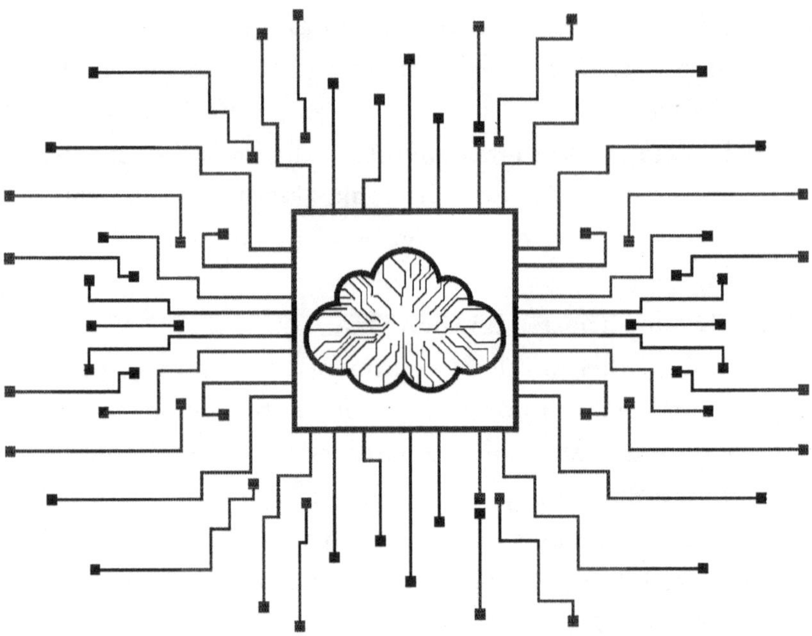

There are various models and techniques for migrating to the cloud, each tailored to meet an organization's specific needs and goals. Below are some widely used cloud migration models and techniques:

Lift and Shift:

This method entails transferring an application or infrastructure from an on-site environment directly to the cloud with minimal to no changes. This approach is straightforward and efficient, but it might not fully exploit the capabilities that cloud computing offers. Lift and shift, also known as rehosting, is especially useful when an organization wishes to move quickly and is perhaps looking to avoid the complexities involved with modifying applications.

The process of lift and shift generally involves these steps:

1. **Selection of Assets for Migration:** This critical first step involves identifying which parts of the infrastructure or which applications are destined for the cloud. It could be anything from physical servers and storage to software systems and network setups.
2. **Analysis of the Selected Assets:** After identifying what will be moved, it's essential to perform a thorough assessment. This is where an organization would look at the application's design or the server's specs to ensure they're suitable for the cloud environment, considering factors like system dependencies and the level of performance required.
3. **Replicating the application or infrastructure in the cloud:** Once the initial analysis confirms compatibility, the next task is to replicate the environment within the cloud. For instance, if moving a virtual machine that hosts an active directory, the organization would set up a corresponding Virtual Machine in the cloud with the necessary configurations to replicate the roles and functions of the original system.
4. **Verification of the Migration:** After replication, testing the migrated entities is paramount to confirm that they operate as expected. Any discrepancies or performance issues would need to be addressed to ensure that the cloud version performs at least as well as the original.

The main benefit of "Lift and Shift" is the quick migration path it offers. Businesses can start using cloud resources sooner, sometimes with minimal downtime. However, this method may not optimize the cost savings or performance enhancements the cloud can offer. For example, simply replicating a resource-intensive application to the cloud without any changes may overlook the opportunity to use more cost-effective services like auto-scaling or to refactor the application to a serverless model, which could be more efficient and economical in the long run.

Choosing "Lift and Shift" necessitates a careful balance between the need for quick migration and the desire to maximize the cloud's potential. This decision is not just about immediate benefits but also about how it aligns with the long-term goals of scalability, manageability, and cost-efficiency.

Replatforming:

Replatforming, commonly referred to as the "lift, tinker, and shift" approach, is a strategy for cloud migration that entails making only essential adjustments to an application or infrastructure to ensure it operates effectively in a cloud setting. This method is typically employed when an application or infrastructure necessitates certain alterations to run in the cloud, yet a complete overhaul would be prohibitively costly or require too much time.

Here's a detailed look at the replatforming process:

1. **Selection of Assets for Migration:** Organizations begin by determining which applications or systems are suitable for moving to the cloud. These might include databases, server-based applications, and other components of IT infrastructure.
2. **Compatibility Assessment:** The next step is a thorough review of the chosen systems to understand how well they will fit into a cloud setting. For instance, examining the database to ensure it supports the cloud's storage and retrieval methods or checking if the current application can scale horizontally in the cloud.
3. **Modifying the application or infrastructure:** Once the review is complete, necessary adjustments are made to the application or system. This could mean altering the code to improve

cloud compatibility, updating middleware to versions that are optimized for the cloud, or adjusting the system's configuration for better integration with cloud services.

4. **Replicating the application or infrastructure in the cloud:** Following the adjustments, the modified version is set up in the cloud. For example, a web server might be moved to a cloud instance that's pre-configured with the right operating system and network settings to match the legacy environment.
5. **Verification of the Migration:** After the move, rigorous testing is conducted to confirm that the application or system performs as expected in its new cloud environment. Any issues found during testing must be resolved to ensure a smooth operation post-migration.

Replatforming's key advantage is its potential to improve an application or system's cloud efficiency without the need for extensive changes. For instance, an e-commerce platform that previously ran on dedicated servers can be replatformed to use cloud-based services for queue management and data storage, which can potentially enhance performance and reduce costs.

However, there are also trade-offs. While less resource-intensive than re-architecting, replatforming may not tap into the full range of cloud functionalities. For example, an application might be moved to the cloud but not re-designed to use auto-scaling features, resulting in missed opportunities for efficiency gains. Moreover, some systems may not be suitable for a simple replatforming if they require significant reconfiguration to work in a cloud environment.

In conclusion, replatforming is a pragmatic approach to cloud migration, offering a balance between quick transfers and optimizing cloud benefits. Organizations should weigh their specific requirements and long-term goals when considering replatforming as their chosen migration technique.

Re-architecting:

This method involves a comprehensive overhaul of applications or infrastructure to leverage cloud-native features like serverless computing, containerization, or the use of microservices. This strategy can require a considerable investment of time and resources but can lead to substantial cost efficiency and performance enhancements. Also known as refactoring, this cloud migration strategy involves making profound alterations to an application or system to tailor it for cloud-native functionalities and design standards. It's particularly relevant for applications or systems that are incompatible with the cloud or require major modifications to harness the full suite of cloud benefits.

Re-architecting includes these critical phases:

1. **Selection of Assets for Migration:** Identifying the components of the IT landscape that will benefit from a cloud-native approach, such as applications that can leverage elasticity or those requiring significant scaling capabilities.
2. **Analysis of the Selected Assets:** A deep evaluation is performed to understand how the application or infrastructure will transition into the cloud, considering the changes needed to align with cloud best practices and functionalities.
3. **Redesigning application or infrastructure:** Based on the assessment, applications or infrastructures are re-envisioned to utilize cloud-native capabilities, such as breaking down a monolithic application into a set of microservices or shifting to a serverless architecture to enhance scalability and reduce operational overhead.
4. **Implementing the redesigned application or infrastructure:** Implementing the re-architected solution using cloud services, for instance, transitioning from a traditional relational database to a cloud-based managed database service that offers scalability and high availability without the overhead of manual management.

5. **Verification of the Migration:** Ensuring the newly migrated solution functions seamlessly in the cloud environment by conducting extensive testing, potentially involving load testing to evaluate performance under various conditions.

The re-architecting process can lead to considerable benefits, such as when an organization transitions a critical application to a microservices architecture, resulting in improved scalability and resilience. It allows the application to leverage on-demand resource allocation, thus reducing costs during off-peak times while managing higher loads effectively during peak times.

On the downside, re-architecting is often a resource-intensive process, both in time and budget, requiring a significant upfront investment. The complexity of re-architecting might not suit all types of applications, especially those with extensive legacy code that cannot be easily decomposed into cloud-native services. Moreover, the expertise required for such a transformation may involve training for existing staff or hiring new talent with specialized skills.

In deciding whether to pursue re-architecting, organizations must weigh the long-term benefits against the immediate costs and potential disruptions. The decision should align with the strategic goals, whether it's achieving operational agility, reducing costs, or scaling more effectively.

Hybrid Cloud:

This method involves a strategic approach where certain applications or infrastructure are transferred to the cloud, while others are retained onsite. The objective is to create a cohesive system that allows both environments to function seamlessly together. This strategy lets organizations enjoy the cloud's flexibility and cost-effectiveness without relinquishing control over their most sensitive applications and data.

In a hybrid cloud migration, an organization selectively moves some of its technological assets to a cloud platform, while others continue to reside within its local data center. The key is to ensure these different components can communicate and operate in unison. This kind of setup offers the benefits of the cloud, such as scalability and remote accessibility, while allowing the retention of critical systems in a private, controlled environment.

The steps to achieve a hybrid cloud setup are:

1. **Selection of Assets for Migration:** The initial task is to decide which components are suitable for cloud relocation and which should stay on-premises due to regulatory, security, or technical reasons.
2. **Analysis of the Selected Assets:** Following selection, a thorough examination is conducted to ensure that the chosen applications or infrastructure will perform optimally in a cloud setting, checking configurations, interdependencies, and performance metrics.
3. **Choosing the right cloud services:** After assessing needs, the next decision is about which cloud services are the most appropriate, whether it be IaaS for base-level infrastructure, PaaS for platform-level support, or SaaS for on-demand software.
4. **Connecting the on-premises and cloud environments:** This stage involves setting up secure communication channels between the on-premises data center and the cloud environment. Methods to achieve this include employing a virtual private network (VPN), which encrypts data for secure internet transport, or opting for a dedicated connection like AWS Direct Connect, which establishes a private link between the data center and the cloud service.
5. **Replicating the applications or infrastructure in the cloud:** Applications or components designated for the cloud are duplicated within the cloud infrastructure. This replication often involves creating a cloud-based duplicate of the

on-premises setup using virtual machines or containers, ensuring consistency between the two environments.

6. **Testing:** After replication, a thorough testing phase is crucial to confirm that the applications or infrastructure components in the cloud function exactly as they do on-premises, ensuring that all features and services are operating correctly.

One practical instance of hybrid cloud connectivity is seen in healthcare, where patient management systems may remain on-premises due to privacy concerns, while analytical workloads that benefit from larger datasets and increased compute power are migrated to the cloud. The secure connectivity in this case is vital to maintain patient confidentiality while benefiting from cloud scalability.

The primary benefit of this migration model is its ability to merge the cloud's efficiencies, like better scalability and cost-effectiveness, with the control and security of local data management. Additionally, it offers an adaptable infrastructure that can evolve as organizational needs change.

Yet, managing a hybrid cloud can introduce challenges. The complexity of overseeing two distinct environments often necessitates additional network and security measures. Moreover, the disparity between cloud and on-premises technologies might call for different sets of tools and management procedures, adding layers of complexity. Therefore, organizations must thoroughly assess their capabilities and needs before committing to a hybrid cloud migration strategy to ensure that the advantages outweigh the potential complexities.

Multi-Cloud Strategy:

This method entails utilizing several cloud service providers to host distinct applications or infrastructure elements. By doing this, organizations can enhance their disaster recovery plans and sidestep dependence on a single cloud vendor. However, such a strategy can be more demanding in terms of management and might lead to higher operational costs.

A multi-cloud migration plan is an approach that involves the use of different cloud providers to host various applications or infrastructure components. This method leverages the strengths of each cloud provider to meet specific requirements for each workload or application, enhancing redundancy and avoiding reliance on a single vendor.

Key steps in a multi-cloud migration include:

1. **Selection of Assets:** This step involves determining which parts of the infrastructure or which applications are suitable for cloud deployment, and whether any will remain on-premises.
2. **Analysis of the Selected Assets:** Once potential candidates for migration have been identified, a thorough evaluation is conducted to check their readiness and compatibility with various cloud platforms. This includes examining configurations, interdependencies, and performance indicators.
3. **Choosing the right cloud services and providers:** Following the assessment, the next task is to select appropriate cloud services and providers. The choices may range across IaaS, PaaS, and SaaS offerings, and will likely involve multiple vendors to accommodate different aspects of the infrastructure or application portfolio.
4. **Connecting the different cloud environments:** Establishing reliable and secure connectivity between the various cloud platforms is vital. This could involve setting up VPNs, leveraging dedicated connectivity options, or employing specialized multi-cloud network services.
5. **Replicating the applications or infrastructure in the cloud:** The next phase is to replicate the selected applications or infrastructure components across the chosen cloud platforms. Creating virtual machine images or containerized versions of applications that mirror the existing on-premises setup is common practice here.

6. **Testing:** Following replication, a rigorous testing process is essential to verify that the applications or infrastructure operate correctly across the multiple cloud environments.

For instance, a global enterprise might use AWS for its computational needs due to its extensive machine learning services, while relying on Microsoft Azure for office productivity applications, and Google Cloud Platform for its big data analytics because of its real-time data processing capabilities.

The strength of adopting a multi-cloud approach is the freedom it gives organizations to avoid dependency on a single vendor and to optimize their applications by selecting the best cloud environment for each task. This strategy enhances business continuity and increases resilience.

Nonetheless, multi-cloud environments introduce challenges such as increased complexity in managing disparate systems, the need for more sophisticated security solutions, and potential inconsistencies in operational processes across platforms. To manage these challenges, organizations often invest in advanced management tools and expertise. Consequently, careful planning and a clear understanding of the goals and potential difficulties are crucial before implementing a multi-cloud strategy.

Beyond these models, several specific techniques facilitate the transition to cloud services, ranging from manual migration, which requires physically transferring data and applications to a cloud environment, to automated migration, which employs sophisticated software tools to streamline the process.

The choice of migration model and techniques is influenced by the unique needs of each organization, the complexity of their existing IT infrastructure, and their strategic goals for adopting cloud technology.

CHAPTER 6

Replace Model

The Replace Model in cloud migration refers to the strategy where an organization chooses to substitute its current on-premises or legacy applications with brand-new, cloud-native applications specifically tailored for optimal performance in a cloud setting. This approach often involves reimagining applications from the ground up, harnessing the most up-to-date cloud technologies and best practices.

This model is particularly suitable when an organization's existing systems are obsolete or incapable of meeting the evolving business needs, or when an extensive overhaul is necessary to fuel growth and foster innovation. By adopting the Replace Model, companies aim to leverage the inherent benefits of cloud computing—like enhanced scalability, agility, and cost-efficiency—while also tapping into the latest advancements in cloud technology.

Undertaking the Replace Model can be more intricate and demand more resources than simpler methods such as the lift-and-shift or replatforming because it requires developing new applications from zero. Nevertheless, the long-term gains can be substantial, offering heightened performance, scalability, and the flexibility to quickly adapt to market changes, which can be crucial for maintaining a competitive edge.

For example, a retail company with an outdated inventory management system that's not compatible with modern e-commerce workflows may opt for the Replace Model. They could choose to implement a new cloud-native solution like Microsoft Dynamics 365 Commerce, which would be designed to integrate seamlessly with online sales channels, supply chain management, and customer relationship management, all hosted in the cloud for optimal performance and scalability.

When considering the Replace Model for cloud migration, it's important for businesses to thoroughly assess their strategic goals, operational needs, and the potential return on investment. While this path may involve higher upfront costs and a longer timeline, the long-term efficiency and strategic advantages often justify the decision for a complete overhaul and adoption of cloud-native solutions.

In the Replace Model of cloud migration, organizations opt to create entirely new applications or systems designed for the cloud from the ground up instead of shifting their existing ones into a cloud environment. This model is usually the best fit when current systems fail to align with the organization's evolving demands or substantial modifications are required to fuel growth and spur innovation.

Crafting new applications for the cloud from the beginning is a more demanding and lengthy process compared to more straightforward strategies such as lift-and-shift or replatforming. This is primarily because it entails conceptualizing and building applications or systems that are fine-tuned for the cloud, rather than merely transferring existing ones to a new setting.

Embarking on this route requires a significant dedication of time, effort, and expertise in both software development and the specifics of cloud technology. However, this investment can yield considerable long-term advantages, enhancing performance, scale, and adaptability, and enabling organizations to maintain a competitive presence in a dynamic digital world.

For instance, a financial institution that relies on legacy banking software may find that it's not suitable for today's mobile-first consumer expectations. In this scenario, they might use the Replace Model to create a new, cloud-native banking platform using technologies like microservices architecture, containers such as Kubernetes, and leveraging cloud-based databases for improved scalability and performance.

Organizations should carry out a thorough examination of their strategic aims, the intricacies of the systems to be developed, the expertise required for such an undertaking, and the anticipated return on this investment when considering the Replace Model. This evaluation should also encompass the challenges that might emerge, including the necessity for rigorous testing, potential integration issues with other systems, and the maintenance of the new applications.

In sum, the Replace Model is a potent route for organizations wishing to overhaul their IT framework and remain at the forefront of the digital marketplace. It requires a substantial commitment and careful planning but can ultimately lead to significant advancements in an organization's technological capabilities.

The Replace Model in cloud migration comes into play for organizations that find their current applications or systems insufficient for their evolving operational demands or for those looking to foster innovation and keep a competitive edge. Below are instances when this model is beneficial:

1. **Legacy Applications:** For businesses saddled with old software that is unsupported or challenging to maintain, moving to cloud-native applications can ease management and upkeep burdens. For example, an insurance company might replace

a decades-old claims processing system with a cloud-based solution to improve processing times and customer service.

2. **Outdated Systems:** When a company's existing systems fail to keep pace with its requirements, it might opt for modern cloud-based solutions that enhance scalability, performance, and adaptability. A retail business, for instance, could transition from a traditional point-of-sale (POS) system to a cloud-based one to handle increased transaction volumes and integrate seamlessly with online sales channels.
3. **Compliance Requirements:** For organizations under stringent regulatory demands, it may be imperative to shift to cloud-native applications built with compliance as a primary focus. A healthcare provider, faced with HIPAA compliance, might replace its patient records system with a cloud service that offers robust security features and compliance controls.
4. **Digital Transformation:** Companies engaged in digital transformation often need to ditch old systems for cloud-native alternatives that enable rapid innovation and a competitive stance in a technology-driven market. A media company could overhaul its content distribution platforms to leverage cloud computing for better scalability across global markets.
5. **Cost Savings:** It may sometimes be more economical for organizations to move to cloud-native applications due to their scalable nature and potential for reduced operational expenses. A startup might forego traditional infrastructure and jump straight to a cloud-native environment to minimize costs and scale as needed without significant upfront investments.

When facing a scenario where the current infrastructure does not align with an organization's strategic goals, or where significant enhancements are required, the Replace Model serves as an ideal solution. It allows organizations to harness the full potential of cloud computing, ensuring they remain agile, cost-efficient, and at the forefront of technological advancements.

Advantages of the "replace" model for cloud migration:

1. **Optimized for the cloud environment:** Applications developed via the "replace" model are created with the cloud's distinct capabilities in mind, enhancing performance and scalability.
2. **Greater agility and innovation:** Crafting new cloud-native applications gives businesses the leverage to incorporate cutting-edge technologies, fostering innovation and a competitive edge.
3. **Compliance and Security:** Cloud-native applications can be engineered with robust security features and regulatory compliance from the onset, safeguarding data and adhering to industry standards.
4. **Customized Architecture:** Starting from scratch allows for a customized approach to the application's architecture, offering a better fit for the organization's needs and facilitating maintenance.
5. **Cost-effectiveness:** Building anew can be financially advantageous in the long term by avoiding the incremental costs associated with maintaining and updating legacy systems.

Disadvantages of the "replace" model for cloud migration:

1. **Extended Timelines:** The development lifecycle for creating new cloud-native applications is typically longer due to the necessity for thorough planning, development, and testing.
2. **Costly:** The upfront costs can be substantial, requiring investment in skilled personnel and infrastructure.
3. **Complex Integration Processes:** Meshing new cloud-native applications with pre-existing systems can present difficulties, sometimes necessitating specialized solutions and expertise.
4. **Disruption to business operations:** Introducing new applications can disrupt current business activities, especially if the application being replaced is integral to the business workflow.

5. **Learning curve:** Transitioning to new systems may temporarily affect productivity as users acclimate to the new environment, potentially increasing the demand for user support.

In summary, while the "replace" model offers the potential for significant improvements in operational performance and strategic flexibility, it also comes with considerable demands on an organization's time and financial resources. Businesses should perform a comprehensive analysis of their strategic goals against the backdrop of these potential advantages and challenges to ascertain the most appropriate migration path.

CHAPTER 7

Retire Approach

The "retire" method in cloud migration focuses on evaluating the organization's application portfolio and determining which systems are obsolete or redundant. These applications are then phased out or decommissioned rather than being moved to the cloud.

Within many companies, outdated legacy systems linger, often due to concerns about data preservation, intertwined dependencies, or simply a lack of clarity regarding their function or value. The retirement strategy aims to mitigate these concerns by systematically eliminating the unnecessary applications, thereby streamlining the migration process and cutting expenses.

For instance, an organization might discover an old customer relationship management (CRM) system that's been replaced by a more advanced solution like Salesforce but is still running in a limited capacity for a small subset of users. Utilizing the "retire" approach, the company would assess the need for this system, archive any necessary data, and then shut down the old CRM to focus resources on the more efficient, cloud-based solution.

This method proves particularly useful for businesses aiming to optimize their IT infrastructure. It allows for reallocating resources away from outdated systems, minimizing the potential for data breaches or loss due to less maintained systems.

Despite the benefits, retiring systems should be done with caution. Potential issues include disruptions to business activities if the application still has active users, the technicalities of data archiving or transfer, and maintaining compliance with data protection regulations. For example, if an obsolete application contains historical financial data, the company must ensure the data is preserved in accordance with tax and accounting laws before decommissioning the system.

At times, retiring a system may involve significant planning, expertise, and resources to avoid impacting business continuity.

In summary, the "retire" strategy can contribute significantly to an organization's efforts to modernize and economize its IT landscape, but it demands a thoughtful, strategic approach, taking into account the company's specific needs and operational goals.

Organizations turn to the "retire" strategy for cloud migration when they possess applications or systems that have become irrelevant or surplus to requirements. This strategy is particularly relevant in the following scenarios:

1. **Legacy Applications:** Firms may find certain old applications to be obsolete or too cumbersome to maintain. Retiring these can liberate resources for more critical functions. For example, a company might be running an ancient, on-premises database

for archiving purposes, which could be efficiently retired in favor of newer, more secure, and cost-effective cloud storage services like Amazon S3 or Azure Blob Storage.

2. **Redundant systems:** If an organization identifies systems that are no longer essential due to consolidation or improved technologies, retiring these systems can help in trimming operational expenses and de-cluttering the tech environment.
3. **End-of-life systems:** When systems approach their end-of-life stage and lose vendor support or no longer fit the organization's requirements, it may be necessary to retire them. A typical example could be an old version of an enterprise resource planning (ERP) system that's no longer receiving updates and could be replaced by a SaaS solution like SAP S/4HANA Cloud.
4. **Mergers and acquisitions:** After mergers or acquisitions, companies often encounter overlapping IT systems. Retiring duplicate systems can help consolidate tools and reduce overhead. For instance, if two merging companies each use a different CRM system, it might make sense to retire one and unify the company on a single platform.
5. **Cloud Migration:** While migrating to the cloud, it may become evident that certain applications are incompatible with cloud environments or simply unnecessary within the new setup. In such cases, it is pragmatic to retire these applications rather than investing in their migration or revamp.

The "retire" strategy helps organizations streamline their operations by discarding the old, underused, or redundant applications. This process, while beneficial, also demands careful consideration to ensure that the retirement does not disrupt business continuity, that all compliance regulations are met, and that data housed in legacy systems is appropriately archived or migrated. Such a strategic cull of IT assets positions a business for a leaner and more focused utilization of technology.

Advantages of the "retire" approach for cloud migration:

1. **Cost savings:** Discontinuing outdated or unused applications cuts down on expenses for upkeep, licenses, and hardware, leading to significant financial savings.
2. **Simplified IT infrastructure:** Eliminating superfluous applications declutters the IT landscape, simplifying administration and support activities.
3. **Reduced risk:** Decommissioning applications that are out-of-date or unsupported mitigates the dangers of data breaches or loss, securing the IT environment.
4. **Improved efficiency:** Redirecting resources from redundant applications to strategic areas can bolster operational efficiency and productivity.
5. **Compliance:** By discontinuing applications that aren't in use, businesses can more easily adhere to legal and industry standards, dodging penalties for noncompliance.

Disadvantages of the "retire" approach for cloud migration:

1. **Business disruption:** Shutting down key applications can interrupt business processes, demanding careful planning to avoid downtime.
2. **Data Loss Risk:** Without meticulous data backup and transition protocols, retiring systems might lead to irreversible data loss.
3. **Dependency Issues:** Some applications are intertwined with other systems. Their retirement could inadvertently affect those reliant on them, creating operational hiccups.
4. **Lack of knowledge:** Sometimes, organizations might not fully understand the extent to which an application is used, leading to hasty decisions that can retire essential systems.
5. **Potential loss of functionality:** Retiring an application could remove unique features that the organization relies on, necessitating the development of alternative solutions.

In conclusion, while the "retire" strategy in cloud migration can lead to a more cost-effective, secure, and streamlined IT framework, it demands a strategic approach. It's crucial to thoroughly assess each system's role and value within the business and to prepare for any contingencies that might arise from its retirement.

CHAPTER 8

Lift/Shift Approach Assessment

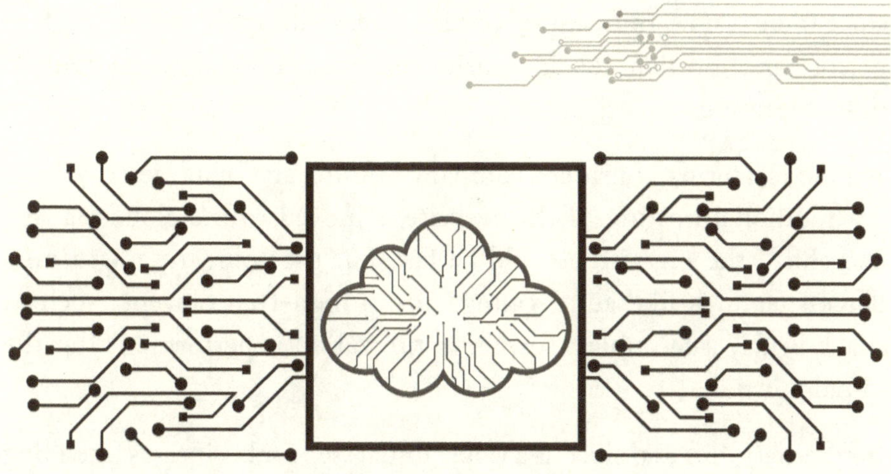

The "lift and shift" method of transitioning to the cloud is a process where existing applications or infrastructures are relocated to the cloud with little alteration. Known also as "rehosting," this process typically involves the transfer of applications or systems from their current on-premises setup to a cloud setting, frequently utilizing automation for efficiency.

Organizations may opt for "lift and shift" for its straightforwardness and rapid deployment since it requires only minimal modification to the current setup. It is particularly fitting for applications and systems that are not tightly coupled with particular hardware or operating systems and can continue to operate in the cloud without substantial reconfiguration.

Key benefits of this strategy include its quick implementation and simplicity. The minimal adjustment needed with "lift and shift" can lead to fewer migration errors and lessen the impact on daily business functions. Furthermore, it provides an entry point to the cloud's scalability, flexibility, and potential cost savings.

Nonetheless, the "lift and shift" approach has its drawbacks. Applications moved in this manner might not fully utilize all cloud capabilities, such as elastic scaling or advanced cloud services. Moreover, since there is no significant re-architecture, some applications may face performance bottlenecks or security concerns that will need attention post-migration.

In practical terms, consider a company running an e-commerce website on traditional hosting. If this website is moved to the cloud via "lift and shift," the migration could be fast, but the company might miss out on features like auto-scaling during high-traffic events such as Black Friday sales, unless further optimization is performed after the initial move.

In summary, "lift and shift" is a viable initial step for businesses intending to migrate promptly to the cloud. However, it's critical to analyze how this move aligns with long-term goals and technical requirements to ensure it's the right decision for the organization's specific needs.

The "lift and shift" strategy is often chosen when a business seeks a swift cloud transition for their applications or systems without substantial modifications. Instances where this might be beneficial include:

1. **Legacy applications:** Companies might find "lift and shift" beneficial for moving older applications to the cloud when these systems don't require specific hardware or operating systems to function. For example, a financial institution using a legacy customer relationship management (CRM) system might move it to the cloud to reduce physical data center reliance without altering the application's core functionality.
2. **Non-Critical Applications:** Applications that play a less crucial role in daily operations and have low complexity are prime

candidates for this approach. An example is a basic document management system used for archival purposes which can be moved without necessitating significant architectural changes.

3. **Development & Testing Environments:** These environments, which are not part of the production workload, can be shifted to the cloud to benefit from quick provisioning and on-demand resources. A tech company could "lift and shift" its software testing environments to replicate production settings without enduring the high costs of an on-premises setup.
4. **Data Backup and Recovery:** Systems designed for backup and archival purposes, which do not require real-time data processing or complex interactions with other systems, can be transitioned smoothly to cloud storage solutions. For instance, a business could transfer its historical data to a cloud service like Amazon Glacier for long-term storage.
5. **Disaster Recovery (DR):** Implementing DR plans using "lift and shift" can significantly enhance recovery time objectives (RTOs) and recovery point objectives (RPOs) by utilizing the cloud's distributed infrastructure. An online retailer, for instance, may shift its DR setup to the cloud to ensure seamless service continuity in case of an outage.

In each case, the main draw is the minimal disruption and fast deployment to the cloud, allowing organizations to leverage cloud benefits more rapidly. Yet, it is vital to consider whether the "lift and shift" method aligns with the long-term digital transformation goals and operational requirements of the business to determine if it is indeed the optimal path forward.

Advantages of the "lift and shift" approach for cloud migration:

1. **Speed:** Migrating via "lift and shift" is a fast process since it involves transferring systems to the cloud without substantial modifications.

2. **Minimal disruption:** This method avoids major changes to systems, thus ensuring business operations continue without significant downtime.
3. **Cost-effective:** It can be a more affordable option upfront because it avoids the expenses related to redesigning or rearchitecting applications.
4. **Flexibility:** This strategy offers the flexibility to migrate to the cloud rapidly and begin enjoying cloud services without redeveloping existing systems.
5. **Retain existing investments:** It allows companies to maintain their current investments in software and technology.

Disadvantages of the "lift and shift" approach for cloud migration:

1. **Limited benefits of cloud:** Migrating without re-architecting may lead to missed opportunities to fully benefit from cloud features like auto-scaling and advanced analytics.
2. **Performance Challenges:** Unaltered architectures may not perform optimally in a cloud setting, potentially necessitating future adjustments.
3. **Security issues:** Existing security measures may not be sufficient in the cloud context, possibly leading to vulnerabilities if not properly addressed.
4. **Higher costs in the long term:** Without cloud optimization, costs could increase over time due to inefficient resource use.
5. **Technical Debt:** Keeping systems unchanged might result in accumulating technical debt, as they may not integrate well with newer cloud technologies or services.

In conclusion, while "lift and shift" can offer a quick transition to cloud computing, it's essential for businesses to weigh the immediate benefits against potential long-term considerations, such as ongoing costs and the need for future enhancements to ensure the strategy aligns with their broader objectives.

CHAPTER 9

Versioning

Version control during cloud migration is the process of documenting and overseeing different iterations of an application or system as it transitions to a cloud-based environment. This process includes recording alterations in the system's design, data transfer stages, and all other components involved in moving to the cloud.

The significance of version control in cloud migration lies in its ability to maintain a historical record of modifications, which is crucial for troubleshooting, consistency, and efficiency. It helps organizations trace the evolution of their applications or systems, pinpoint discrepancies or bugs promptly, and rectify them before they escalate.

A variety of instruments and technological solutions are available to aid in versioning during cloud migration. These include version control systems, tools for managing configurations, and automation tools for testing and deployment. Utilizing these tools can simplify the migration workflow and guarantee that modifications are documented and handled systematically and effectively.

Version control is a crucial component of cloud migration. It ensures that every change is documented, provides a rollback path in case of errors, and supports a systematic and coherent transition process. By leveraging the right tools, organizations can enhance their oversight and efficiency during migration, ensuring a smoother and more reliable transition to the cloud.

Version control is a critical component in the process of cloud migration, closely monitoring and cataloging different iterations of an application or system during the shift. This process includes keeping a detailed log of alterations to the system's structure, the data transfer progression, and other key migration stages. The adoption of version control is instrumental in maintaining a uniform and streamlined transition, allowing for swift identification and resolution of any issues, thus preventing minor hitches from turning into significant setbacks.

In the multifaceted endeavor of moving to the cloud, where considerations such as security, compliance, scalability, and cost must be addressed, version control acts as an organizational compass. It ensures that every change to the application or system is carefully considered and documented, offering a structured methodology to manage the inherent complexities of migration.

Tools like Git provide robust version control systems that help track code changes, while configuration management tools such as Ansible enable precise infrastructure setups. Furthermore, continuous integration and deployment services like Jenkins automate testing and deployment, maintaining the application in a consistent state throughout the migration.

Once the migration is underway or completed, version control continues to deliver value by facilitating the ongoing upkeep and evolution of the application in the cloud environment. It offers a systematic approach to incremental updates and maintenance, ensuring that each version of the application is functional, secure, and optimized for performance.

In essence, version control is indispensable for orchestrating a successful cloud migration journey. It not only simplifies the initial move but also underpins the future growth and development of the application in its new cloud habitat.

Versioning plays a crucial role in the process of transitioning applications or systems to the cloud for multiple reasons:

1. **Consistency:** It ensures a methodical approach where all modifications are carefully logged and handled, promoting a uniform migration process.
2. **Risk Reduction:** Keeping track of various iterations of the application or system aids in promptly spotting potential problems during migration, enabling organizations to proactively address them.
3. **Collaboration:** With a central record of all updates, teams find it simpler to work together on the migration, reducing the likelihood of miscommunication or overlap in changes.
4. **Maintenance:** As applications or systems evolve in the cloud, versioning assists in tracking changes, simplifying the process of troubleshooting and enhancing the system post-migration.
5. **Compliance:** It provides a framework for maintaining an audit trail of all changes, which is critical for proving compliance with various industry regulations.

The significance of versioning extends beyond the migration phase. For instance, in the financial sector, where firms are required to maintain rigorous change logs for audits, tools like Subversion or Mercurial can be vital. Or, in software development companies, where multiple teams may be updating services, a tool like GitHub provides a collaborative environment with comprehensive version control.

If versioning is not done during cloud migration, there are several risks that organizations may face:

1. **Data Loss:** An absence of proper change logging can lead to mishaps where critical data is overwritten or lost, complicating the migration.
2. **Increased risk of errors:** A lack of version tracking may result in uncaught errors proliferating through the system, leading to potential failure in the cloud.
3. **Inconsistency:** Without a structured versioning process, achieving a consistent migration across multiple systems becomes challenging, which could lead to unpredictable system behavior.
4. **Difficulty in managing changes:** Keeping up with and managing ongoing changes post-migration could become cumbersome and error-prone without a version history.
5. **Compliance issues:** For organizations subject to regulations, an inability to present a clear history of changes could result in legal penalties or fines.

In conclusion, versioning serves as an indispensable tool for a smooth and secure cloud migration, underpinning not just the initial move but also the long-term management and compliance of the application or system within its new cloud-based ecosystem.

PHASE 2

DATABASE MAPPING WITH APPLICATIONS

CHAPTER 10

Database Mapping with Applications

Database mapping is a critical step in cloud migration, involving a thorough analysis of how applications interact with their databases. It's essential because applications often depend on databases to function correctly, and any change in the application's environment, like a move to the cloud, entails a corresponding change in its database setup.

This mapping process requires an in-depth look at the databases linked to each application, identifying specific data tables and elements the application uses. Armed with this information, teams can chart out a detailed plan to transition both the applications and their databases to the cloud, ensuring that they continue to work in tandem just as they did in the on-premises setup.

The complexity of database mapping varies, particularly with applications that draw from several databases or have intricate data relationships. Despite these complexities, it's a vital part of the migration journey. Incorrect mapping could lead to data being misplaced, lost, or corrupted, which could derail the application's functionality in the cloud.

For example, a retail company with a robust e-commerce platform might need to migrate its customer-facing application to the cloud. As part of this process, they must map out the various databases that hold customer data, inventory information, and transaction records. Each of these databases has to be carefully aligned with the application in the cloud to ensure seamless service post-migration.

In conclusion, meticulous database mapping is indispensable for successful cloud migration. It helps safeguard data integrity, maintains application performance, and avoids the pitfalls that come with data-related discrepancies post-migration.

Database mapping with applications during cloud migration is a key process that identifies how applications interact with their databases. This task is crucial because it directly impacts the ability of the applications to function correctly post-migration. The database mapping process typically involves several steps:

1. **Identify applications and databases:** The initial step is to pinpoint which applications and databases are interconnected. It's about understanding the architecture and how the components of the application and the database communicate with each other.
2. **Map tables and data elements:** After establishing which applications and databases are linked, the focus shifts to the specific tables and data elements within the databases that the application depends on. This step involves identifying which data is crucial for the operation of the application and how these pieces of data are related.

3. **Evaluate compatibility:** With a clear map of the data and its elements, it's then necessary to evaluate how the database will fit into the cloud environment. This step identifies any potential compatibility issues that might emerge during the database migration and formulates strategies to resolve them.
4. **Strategizing the Migration:** The final stage is to craft a comprehensive migration strategy for both the application and its associated database(s). Decisions are made based on data volume, the intricacy of the migration, and how much downtime can be tolerated.

The intricacies of database mapping escalate with the complexity of the application's reliance on multiple databases or sophisticated data structures. Despite these challenges, meticulous mapping is indispensable for a smooth transition. Improper mapping can lead to severe consequences such as data loss or corruption. For instance, a healthcare provider with an electronic health record (EHR) system might need to map out patient records, appointment schedules, and billing information. Each category of data might reside in different databases or tables that need careful migration to ensure that the EHR system functions seamlessly in the cloud.

In essence, database mapping is foundational for ensuring that applications and their associated data make the transition to the cloud environment effectively and cohesively. It's about making informed decisions that uphold business continuity while harnessing the advantages of cloud computing.

CHAPTER 11

Clustering

Clustering in cloud migration refers to the practice of organizing servers or instances into groups that share similar characteristics or workloads. This approach is particularly useful in cloud computing to enhance performance, ensure high availability, and balance workloads effectively.

In the journey to the cloud, clustering is a strategic move that can significantly influence the efficiency of the infrastructure. It ensures that applications or systems moving to the cloud are supported by a backend that can handle their specific demands. For example, an online retail company may cluster their transaction processing servers separately from their content delivery servers, ensuring that both customer-facing speed and backend processing power are optimized.

Effective clustering involves categorizing servers based on factors such as the type of workload they handle, their performance metrics, and availability needs. This allows for a more precise allocation of resources, preventing scenarios where some servers are overwhelmed while others lay idle. As a result, not only is performance enhanced, but organizations can also be more cost-efficient by avoiding the wastage of resources.

Moreover, clustering contributes to scalability in the cloud. It enables organizations to dynamically adjust their resources in response to fluctuating demands. For instance, during peak periods, a media streaming service can add more servers to its content delivery cluster to maintain smooth streaming quality for a growing number of users.

Clustering is a vital process in cloud migration that aids businesses in tailoring their cloud infrastructure for optimal performance, ensuring high availability, and maintaining the flexibility to scale as needed. By grouping servers thoughtfully, companies can achieve a high-performing cloud environment that aligns with their operational demands and is cost-effective in the long run.

The clustering process typically involves several steps:

1. **Identify clustering criteria:** The process begins with determining the basis for clustering, which could be the nature of the workload, performance specifications, and required uptime.
2. **Collect performance data:** Next, it's crucial to gather data on the servers' performance. Metrics might include CPU usage, network throughput, and disk input/output operations.
3. **Analyze data:** Analyzing the collected data is the subsequent step, possibly involving advanced techniques like machine learning to discern patterns or correlations among the performance indicators.
4. **Cluster servers or instances:** With the analysis in hand, servers or instances are then grouped according to the established criteria, ensuring that similar workloads are managed collectively.
5. **Evaluate and refine:** The last step is a continuous evaluation of the clustering efficiency, followed by necessary refinements. Performance data is monitored regularly to adapt the clustering strategy to any changes in workload behavior or system requirements.

This methodical approach to clustering is integral to managing a cloud environment efficiently. It allows for resource allocation that is both demand-responsive and cost-effective. For instance, an IT service provider may cluster its web servers separately from its database servers to ensure each group is optimized for its specific workload requirements without interference from the other.

In conclusion, clustering in cloud computing is a strategic process that, when executed thoughtfully, ensures that an organization's cloud infrastructure is not only performance-driven but also scalable and flexible to adapt to changing demands.

What are some of the scenarios when clustering is not recommended

Clustering in the cloud is a powerful tool for enhancing system efficiency, but there are situations where it might not be the best course of action. Here are some instances where clustering might not be advisable:

1. **Low workload demand:** For applications or systems with consistently low workload demands, clustering could introduce unnecessary complexity without any tangible benefits, as the existing resources might be sufficient to handle the load.
2. **High resource utilization:** In a scenario where the existing servers or instances are already running at full capacity, clustering them could worsen performance issues, as it would not address the fundamental problem of resource limitation.
3. **Non-distributed workloads:** Applications or systems that do not distribute their workload across multiple servers might not benefit from clustering. For instance, a single-instance database used for a specific function may not see performance improvements through clustering.
4. **Legacy applications:** Older applications or systems may not support clustering due to outdated technology or architecture constraints. Attempting to cluster such systems could lead to complications or failures, negating any potential clustering benefits.

5. **Compliance requirements:** Certain applications with stringent data security and privacy regulations may not be suitable for clustering. Clustering could potentially increase the risk of data breaches if not managed with the necessary security protocols.

It's essential for organizations to assess their specific needs against the potential risks and rewards of clustering. Factors such as workload patterns, resource usage, system architecture, and compliance mandates should all be weighed to determine if clustering will truly serve the organization's objectives in the cloud.

Here are some tips for effective clustering process in cloud computing:

1. **Identify clustering criteria:** Define clear criteria for how you will group your servers or instances. Consider elements like the nature of the workload, performance expectations, and required uptime to ensure like-with-like grouping.
2. **Collect performance data:** It's crucial to collect detailed performance data from your infrastructure. Metrics such as CPU usage, network activity, and disk operations will give you insights into how to best configure your clusters.
3. **Analyze data:** Once you have your performance data, thoroughly analyze it to spot patterns and correlations. Tools that employ machine learning algorithms can be particularly useful in uncovering these insights.
4. **Test and refine:** Before going live, test your clustering strategy in a non-production environment. This allows you to fine-tune your approach. Continuous monitoring for performance after deployment is also key to maintaining effective clustering.
5. **Consider automation:** Use automation tools to make the clustering process more reliable and efficient. Automation scripts and configuration management tools can help streamline clustering and reduce the potential for mistakes.

6. **Implement failover mechanisms:** High availability is critical. Design your clusters with failover capabilities to handle potential system failures without significant downtime, using solutions like load balancers to distribute traffic and workloads evenly.

Effective clustering plays a crucial role in enhancing performance, ensuring availability, and scaling in the cloud. By meticulously determining the criteria for clustering, gathering and evaluating performance metrics, iterating on the clustering approach through testing, and establishing failover protocols, businesses can optimize their infrastructure to meet their application or system demands.

PHASE 3

MOBILIZING PHASE

CHAPTER 12

Mobilizing Overview

The mobilizing phase is the critical first leg of the cloud migration journey, setting the stage for the organization's transition to cloud computing. In this phase, businesses assess their readiness for adopting the cloud, evaluate their technical and business prerequisites, explore suitable cloud services, and map out a comprehensive plan for the migration.

Key activities in the mobilizing phase include:

1. **Cloud Readiness Assessment:** This step involves scrutinizing the organization's readiness for the cloud transition by examining technical needs, potential risks, and devising strategies to address them.
2. **Cloud provider evaluation:** The organization must choose a cloud provider that aligns with its needs, considering aspects such as service performance, security measures, and cost

structures. For instance, a company might weigh the offerings of Google Cloud against AWS, examining how each platform's features fit with their operational needs.

3. **Cloud migration planning:** Crafting a detailed migration plan is next, pinpointing critical milestones, setting timelines, and recognizing dependencies. Essential resources and personnel required for the migration are also identified during this phase.
4. **Cloud cost analysis:** A thorough analysis of all expenses related to the migration and subsequent cloud operations is conducted. This includes infrastructure expenses, software licensing, and data transfer fees.
5. **Cloud migration team formation:** The final step is assembling a team capable of carrying out the migration. This includes internal IT personnel, potentially augmented by external consultants and representatives from the chosen cloud service provider.

By diligently navigating these steps, an organization can confidently prepare for cloud adoption, ensuring they have a robust strategy and the right team in place. This preparation is vital to smoothly progress to the executing phase of the cloud migration process.

CHAPTER 13

RACI and Detailed Plan

Defining a RACI (Responsible, Accountable, Consulted, Informed) matrix is a vital step in the cloud migration process. It serves to delineate clear roles and duties, ensuring that every stakeholder understands their specific contributions to the migration effort. The following are key actions to establish a RACI matrix for cloud migration:

1. **Identify stakeholders:** Start by listing everyone involved in the cloud migration effort. This group could range from your internal IT department and project managers to external cloud consultants and service providers. Each stakeholder's role should be clearly identified to cover all bases of the migration project.
2. **Define tasks and activities:** Detail every task required for the migration. This should be comprehensive, from the initial

assessment and selection of workloads for migration to the actual data transfer and the eventual decommissioning of legacy systems.

3. **Assign RACI roles:** After defining the tasks and activities, the next step is to assign RACI roles to each stakeholder for each task or activity. The RACI roles are as follows:

    3.1 **Responsible:** Assign individuals or teams who will be doing the work for each task. For example, IT personnel may be responsible for the actual data migration, while the application team handles software compatibility checks.

    3.2 **Accountable:** Designate who has the final say and where the buck stops for each task. Often, this will be project leads or department heads. For instance, the CTO or IT Director may be accountable for the overall success of the migration.

    3.3 **Consulted:** Identify experts or stakeholders whose input is valuable for task completion. These might be network architects for infrastructure setup or legal advisors for compliance matters.

    3.4 **Informed:** List those who need updates on progress but aren't actively involved in task execution, such as department leads outside of IT, or perhaps the finance department for budget-related updates.

4. **Review and finalize:** Review the drafted RACI matrix with all involved stakeholders to confirm understanding and agreement on the assigned roles and responsibilities. This step prevents any overlap or confusion during the migration process.

By thoroughly working through these steps, you'll establish a clear, shared understanding among all parties involved in the migration. This clarity is crucial for a smooth transition to the cloud and helps prevent any missteps or confusion during the process.

What are some of the main roles in cloud migration and their RACI

In the context of cloud migration, distinct roles are carved out, each with specific RACI-chart responsibilities to streamline the transition process:

1. **Cloud Migration Manager:**

   1.1 Takes charge of the cloud migration end-to-end management.
   1.2 Holds the ultimate responsibility for the migration project's success, making key decisions and providing oversight.
   1.3 Is a key figure for consultation on the migration's strategic direction and decision-making.
   1.4 Stays informed on all progress and updates, ensuring the migration stays on track.

2. **Cloud Architect:**

   2.1 Designs the overall cloud environment architecture, including considerations for scalability, reliability, and security.
   2.2 Is accountable for the cloud architecture's integrity and its alignment with business and technical requirements.
   2.3 Offers expert guidance to IT teams and stakeholders on cloud solutions and best practices.
   2.4 Receives regular updates to verify that the architecture implementation adheres to the planned design.

3. **Application Owner:**

   3.1 Identifies and prioritizes applications for migration to the cloud, ensuring they align with business priorities.
   3.2 Is accountable for the successful transition of their applications, ensuring functionality and performance in the cloud.
   3.3 Provides detailed insights during consultations to ensure the application's requirements are met in the new environment.
   3.4 Gets updates on the migration progress, addressing any concerns related to their applications.

4. **IT Operations:**

   4.1 Executes the deployment and ongoing management of the cloud infrastructure.
   4.2 Is accountable for operational performance, ensuring the infrastructure supports all migrated services effectively.
   4.3 Offers operational insights and is consulted on issues related to infrastructure management.
   4.4 Is kept up-to-date on the operational status, any challenges encountered, and the resolution of those issues.

5. **Security and Compliance:**

   5.1 Ensures that the migration project adheres to all relevant security protocols and compliance mandates.
   5.2 Is accountable for the cloud infrastructure's security posture, addressing vulnerabilities, and maintaining compliance.
   5.3 Provides expertise on security and compliance matters during planning and execution stages.
   5.4 Receives regular briefings on the status of security measures and any compliance-related concerns.

6. **Project Sponsor:**

   6.1 Provides the financial resources and high-level support necessary for the cloud migration endeavor.
   6.2 Carries the responsibility for the migration's alignment with the broader business goals and strategic directives.
   6.3 Offers wisdom and high-level direction to the project team, ensuring alignment with business strategy.
   6.4 Receives consistent updates on the progress of the migration effort to track investment performance and project alignment with business expectations.

The clarity provided by the RACI matrix ensures that everyone involved understands their specific role within the project, which is critical for managing a structured and effective migration to the cloud. This clarity of roles is especially crucial in complex migrations, where multiple departments and external vendors may be involved.

When orchestrating a cloud migration, the involvement of extended and vendor teams is often indispensable, and their roles must be integrated into the RACI matrix to avoid overlaps and gaps in responsibility.

1. **Extended Teams:** These teams might include staff from departments such as compliance, finance, legal, or human resources. Their role in the cloud migration process often revolves around providing specialized knowledge and ensuring that the migration adheres to industry standards, financial constraints, legal regulations, and HR policies. They are typically consulted for their expert opinion and kept informed about relevant decisions and outcomes.
2. **Vendor Teams:** Teams from external service providers, offering cloud services or other resources essential for the migration, play a crucial part in the process. Depending on the contract and scope of services, vendor teams might be responsible for implementing certain technologies or accountable for the performance and reliability of cloud services provided. Their role is to work hand in hand with internal teams to support the technical aspects of the migration.

The RACI matrix, in this context, serves as a blueprint for collaboration. It details the involvement and expectations from both internal and external teams, ensuring that the migration process is cohesive and that each contributor is aware of their specific duties. This strategic alignment is essential for the smooth execution and completion of a cloud migration project.

What is a detailed plan for cloud migration?

Developing a thorough cloud migration plan is similar to drawing a detailed map for a complex journey. It delineates every aspect of the migration process, covering which assets will move to the cloud, the migration's intent, and the logistical specifics. Here's what such a plan typically encompasses:

1. **Project Scope:** This component specifies which applications, data sets, and services are slated for cloud transition. It also highlights dependencies and necessary integrations between various elements.
2. **Migration Goals and Objectives:** Here, the organization defines what it aims to achieve with the cloud migration, whether it's enhancing flexibility, expanding scalability, or achieving cost-efficiency.
3. **Cloud Deployment Model:** The plan specifies the chosen cloud environment—be it public, private, hybrid, or multi-cloud—that aligns with the organization's strategic and operational needs.
4. **Cloud Service Provider Selection:** This involves a critical evaluation to select a cloud service provider that aligns with organizational criteria, considering factors like cost structures, service performance, security protocols, and adherence to regulatory compliance.
5. **Migration Timeline:** A detailed schedule of milestones and deadlines is essential, highlighting key dates and events that the migration must synchronize with.
6. **Resource Requirements:** Identifying what resources are necessary for the migration, this section outlines the need for personnel, technological infrastructure, and network capabilities.
7. **Migration Methods:** The plan describes the specific strategies and tools that will be utilized for the cloud migration, detailing whether approaches like lift and shift, replatforming, or rearchitecting will be employed.
8. **Testing and Validation:** It includes steps to ensure the migrated systems perform optimally and meet all necessary security and compliance benchmarks.

9. **Employee and Stakeholder Training:** This ensures that everyone involved is up-to-date with the new cloud environment and any procedural changes.

Ongoing Monitoring and Management: The plan outlines procedures for continuous oversight of the cloud environment to maintain performance and compliance and to carry out necessary optimizations and cost management activities.

Why is it needed?

A well-crafted plan for cloud migration is a linchpin for success, addressing several critical areas:

1. **Minimizing disruptions:** A meticulously crafted plan aims to keep business interruption at bay. By conducting a thorough assessment of the current IT setup, identifying potential snags or interdependencies, the organization can take preemptive measures to tackle challenges, ensuring the migration doesn't hinder day-to-day operations.
2. **Ensuring security and compliance:** It's imperative to ensure that migration doesn't compromise security or flout regulatory requirements. Early identification of security protocols and compliance mandates within the planning phase enables organizations to weave these considerations into their migration strategy, safeguarding data throughout the process.
3. **Managing costs:** With a clear-eyed view of the resources and approaches required for migration, a detailed plan also serves as a financial compass. It guides the organization in budgeting, preventing cost overruns by aligning the migration expenses with the organization's financial objectives.
4. **Streamlining the migration process:** The plan acts as a blueprint for the migration journey, setting out each phase clearly. Defining timelines, allocating resources, and detailing the steps to be taken enhances the efficiency and effectiveness of the entire migration process.

5. **Improving communication and collaboration:** A good plan lays out a collaborative framework for all parties involved in the migration. It assigns clear-cut roles and responsibilities, sets expectations, and establishes communication protocols, which can significantly enhance synergy and ensure everyone is pulling in the same direction towards the shared end goal.

In essence, a detailed cloud migration plan is not just a roadmap but also a tool for risk mitigation, cost management, and team alignment, all of which contribute to a successful transition into the cloud infrastructure.

What types of costs need to be considered?

Creating a comprehensive cloud migration plan necessitates accounting for various financial implications to avoid budget overruns and ensure a cost-effective transition:

1. **Migration costs:** These are the costs related to the actual process of moving digital assets to the cloud. They can range from fees for migration services and tools to the expenses incurred in data transfer and labor costs for the technical team carrying out the migration.
2. **Infrastructure Costs:** This includes the costs of the cloud resources themselves, like processing power, data storage, bandwidth, and any additional services for maintaining security and compliance standards.
3. **Operational Costs:** Post-migration, there are ongoing expenses for the day-to-day running of cloud services. This category covers operational staff, routine maintenance, support services, and any software licenses needed for the cloud environment.
4. **Training Costs:** Transitioning to the cloud often requires upskilling the workforce to navigate the new systems efficiently. The associated costs might include training programs, workshop sessions, and materials to get employees and stakeholders up to speed with the changes.

5. **Performance optimization Costs:** After migration, further investment might be necessary to fine-tune the performance of cloud services. This could involve analyzing and resolving performance issues or implementing solutions like auto-scaling to handle varying workloads efficiently.
6. **Security and Compliance Costs:** Ensuring the cloud setup adheres to the required security and regulatory standards can incur costs related to security software, compliance audits, and certification processes to demonstrate adherence to industry regulations.

CHAPTER 14

RFP Process and Cloud Provider Selection

The RFP (Request for Proposal) process is an established method for organizations to invite proposals from potential cloud service providers for cloud migration or other IT-related services. The RFP document usually details the organization's objectives, specifications, and expected results, asking vendors to submit comprehensive proposals on how they intend to fulfill these requirements.

Selecting a cloud provider entail assessing and picking the service provider(s) that most suitably align with the organization's criteria, considering aspects like pricing, efficiency, security, regulatory adherence, and customer support. The selection procedure typically includes these stages:

Define Selection Criteria:

Establishing a list of parameters against which potential cloud service providers will be assessed. This includes pricing models, system performance benchmarks, security protocols, compliance assurances, and the level of customer support offered.

Establishing the criteria for choosing a cloud provider is an essential part of the selection process, ensuring that the organization assesses prospective cloud service providers on their capability to satisfy the organization's specific needs and prerequisites. Below are several guidelines for determining the selection criteria:

1. **Identify Organizational Needs:** It's crucial to have a clear understanding of the organizational needs for cloud services. This could encompass a range of factors from system uptime and scalability to data sovereignty and industry-specific compliance requirements.
2. **Prioritize the selection criteria:** Not all selection criteria will hold equal weight. Determine which aspects are non-negotiable and which can be compromised on, thus prioritizing them accordingly. For instance, a financial institution may place a higher premium on security features over cost considerations due to regulatory demands.
3. **Define the criteria:** Expand on each criterion to establish the exact specifications expected from providers. If uptime is a criterion, specify the acceptable percentage of uptime required.
4. **Consider multiple perspectives:** Engage with diverse stakeholders within the organization to gather a broad view of what different departments consider critical to their operations.
5. **Keep it simple and clear:** It's imperative that the criteria are straightforward and transparent to ensure they are

understandable not only internally but also by prospective providers who will respond to the RFP.

Develop an RFP:

The formulation of an RFP is a pivotal step for organizations charting their journey to the cloud. It serves as a formal invitation for cloud service providers to present their solutions tailored to the organization's specific cloud migration needs. Here's how to structure this crucial document:

1. **Define the scope:** Begin by delineating the exact requirements for cloud services. This includes not only the technical specifications but also any constraints the organization might face, such as legal, geographical, or industry-specific limitations.
2. **Identify the organization's needs and requirements:** Be explicit about what the organization is looking for in its transition to the cloud. This includes detailing performance expectations, scalability needs, security standards, compliance obligations, support levels, and budget constraints.
3. **Develop the RFP structure:** Organize the RFP into clear sections that guide vendors through the organization's background, the services sought, the criteria for selection, and the submission process.
4. **Define the evaluation criteria:** Articulate the benchmarks and standards that will be used to assess vendor proposals. These should mirror the initial selection criteria to ensure alignment with organizational objectives.
5. **Provide clear instructions:** Offer precise guidance on the proposal submission process, including the format, necessary documentation, and any templates or forms that vendors need to use.
6. **Allow for questions and feedback:** Provide an avenue for vendors to seek clarifications, ask questions, and offer feedback about the RFP content to ensure they fully understand the expectations and can tailor their proposals accordingly.

7. **Establish a timeline:** Set out a clear schedule for all phases of the RFP process, from the initial submission to the final selection, ensuring all parties are cognizant of the deadlines.

Identify potential vendors:

In the journey toward cloud adoption, pinpointing the right vendors is a task that can dictate the success of the migration. It's essential to canvas the market for providers with a solid track record and the specific know-how that aligns with the organization's cloud aspirations. Here are some tips for identifying potential vendors:

1. **Research cloud service providers:** Delve into industry reports, case studies, and customer testimonials to gauge the credibility and strength of cloud service providers. This background check is vital for compiling a list of vendors with industry-proven expertise.
2. **Consider the vendor's expertise:** Scrutinize each vendor's specialization areas. Whether it's cybersecurity measures, regulatory compliance capabilities, or performance optimization, the vendor's strengths should align with the organization's priority needs.
3. **Seek recommendations:** Leverage the experiences of industry counterparts. Recommendations from businesses with similar cloud migration pathways can be invaluable in understanding a vendor's real-world performance.
4. **Attend industry events:** Participate in cloud computing symposiums, webinars, and expos. Such platforms often serve as a showcase for vendors to present their competencies and are excellent for direct queries and networking.
5. **Search online:** Utilize digital channels, including search engines and dedicated cloud service comparison platforms, to discover and assess potential vendors. These resources often provide a wealth of information on service models, pricing structures, and user ratings.

6. **Consider partnerships:** Evaluate whether current partnerships can be extended to include cloud services. Vendors already serving the organization in other capacities might offer seamless integration solutions for cloud services, simplifying the transition.

Evaluate vendor proposals:

Examine the submitted proposals from potential suppliers to identify those who fulfill the established selection criteria and align best with the organization's requirements.

Assessing vendor submissions is a pivotal element in selecting a cloud service provider. It ensures that the organization selects a provider that aligns with their specific needs and criteria. Consider the following advice for assessing vendor submissions:

1. **Review the proposal against the RFP:** Review each vendor's proposal to confirm that it aligns with the stipulations and goals outlined in the RFP. It's essential that the proposal resonates with the organization's articulated cloud migration pathway and objectives.
2. **Evaluate the vendor's experience:** Investigate the vendor's historical performance and domain expertise. It's crucial to select a vendor that not only promises high-caliber services but also has a trail of successful implementations, especially in areas pertinent to your organization's requirements.
3. **Assess the vendor's capabilities:** Review each vendor's proposed solutions for alignment with the organization's technical and strategic demands. Confirm that they offer not just current compatibility but also the scalability and adaptability that will accommodate future growth and evolving needs.
4. **Review pricing and service level agreements (SLAs):** Analyze the cost structure and the service level agreements put forward. The pricing should offer a good return on investment without

compromising on service quality, while SLAs should guarantee the requisite performance standards and remediation measures.

5. **Consider references and testimonials:** Seek out feedback from the vendor's existing clientele to gauge customer service and satisfaction levels. Customer experiences can provide invaluable insights into the vendor's operational effectiveness and reliability.
6. **Evaluate support and training options:** Delve into the vendor's post-migration support infrastructure and their training provisions. Post-deployment support is critical to resolve any emerging issues promptly, and comprehensive training programs are necessary for a smooth transition to the new cloud environment.
7. **Consider security and compliance:** Confirm that the vendor's security protocols and compliance assurances meet or exceed your organization's stringent standards. Given the escalating cyber threats and complex regulatory landscape, the vendor's security and compliance measures are non-negotiable criteria.

Conduct due diligence:

Conduct a comprehensive investigation of the chosen vendors, which includes confirming their qualifications, consulting references, and executing background screenings. Thorough due diligence is a pivotal phase in selecting a cloud service provider, essentially serving as a meticulous vetting process to validate the vendor's capability to meet the organization's cloud migration aspirations. Here is a breakdown of the steps involved:

1. **Credential Verification:** Ensure the vendor holds up-to-date industry credentials and certifications such as SOC 2, ISO 27001, or HIPAA, which can be critical for compliance in sectors like finance or healthcare. For instance, a healthcare organization would need to ensure their chosen vendor, perhaps Google Cloud, possesses the necessary Health

Insurance Portability and Accountability Act (HIPAA) compliance certifications.

2. **Check references and testimonials:** Solicit feedback from the vendor's existing clientele, particularly those with similar scale or industry background, to ascertain their satisfaction levels and the vendor's track record for delivering on promises.
3. **Conduct background checks:** Investigate the vendor's history for any legal, financial, or compliance red flags that could signal potential risk, using both public records and specialized due diligence services.
4. **Review financial stability:** Analyze the vendor's financial reports and market performance to confirm their economic stability and capacity to support long-term service agreements.
5. **Evaluate support and training options:** Probe the depth and breadth of the vendor's customer support and training provisions. Adequate support is critical to resolve operational hiccups post-migration efficiently, while robust training programs are vital for a seamless transition.
6. **Review service level agreements (SLAs):** Examine the vendor's Service Level Agreements to ensure they align with your organization's performance benchmarks and offer fair remediation for any lapses in service delivery.
7. **Assess the vendor's disaster recovery and business continuity plans:** Evaluate the vendor's resilience strategies, including their disaster recovery and business continuity plans. A vendor should have a solid framework for maintaining uptime or rapidly restoring services in the event of a disaster.

Negotiate contracts:

Negotiating contracts with cloud service providers is an intricate process that solidifies the terms under which an organization will migrate to and operate within the cloud. Here is a step-by-step approach to ensure effective contract negotiations:

1. **Establish clear goals and objectives:** Begin with a lucid outline of what the organization aims to achieve through these negotiations, which could include specific service expectations, budgetary constraints, and critical terms that need addressing.
2. **Prioritize the negotiation points:** Rank the terms in order of importance. This helps in focusing efforts on securing favorable conditions on the most critical aspects first, such as data governance or uptime guarantees.
3. **Understand the vendor's pricing and business model:** Gain an in-depth understanding of the vendor's pricing model. For example, if considering Amazon Web Services (AWS), it's crucial to negotiate terms based on anticipated data usage and scalability needs, aligning with AWS's pay-as-you-go pricing structure.
4. **Negotiate Service Level Agreements (SLAs):** SLAs are the crux of the contract. Negotiate SLAs that match the organization's uptime requirements and include clear metrics for performance, along with penalties for SLA breaches.
5. **Consider security and compliance requirements:** Ensure that the contract terms meet the organization's stringent security and regulatory compliance needs. This might include the right to audit, data encryption standards, and adherence to specific regulations like GDPR.
6. **Review termination and renewal terms:** Clarify the terms around contract termination, including notice periods, liabilities, and data retention policies post-termination. This ensures that the organization is not locked into unfavorable long-term commitments.
7. **Work collaboratively with the vendor:** Approach negotiations as a collaborative effort to reach a mutually beneficial agreement. Maintaining a flexible stance can often lead to more favorable outcomes.

Implement and manage the cloud environment:

Implementing and managing a cloud environment is a comprehensive process crucial to the successful adoption and operation of cloud services. Organizations must ensure the cloud infrastructure is set up to meet their needs and that they have procedures in place for ongoing oversight and optimization. Here's an expanded approach:

1. **Develop a detailed implementation plan:** Outline each step required to transition to the cloud, specifying actions such as application migration, setting up cloud services, and establishing connectivity requirements. This plan should be granular, noting each milestone, deliverable, and the timeline for achieving them.
2. **Ensure proper security and compliance:** Configure security settings to protect data and applications in the cloud environment rigorously. This includes implementing encryption, access controls, and regular audits to ensure compliance with industry regulations and internal policies.
3. **Implement monitoring and management tools:** Utilize advanced tools for continuous monitoring of cloud resources to ensure optimal performance and security. These tools should provide actionable insights into resource utilization, system health, and potential security threats.
4. **Develop operational processes and procedures:** Develop new processes or adapt existing ones for cloud operations, including data backups, disaster recovery, resource scaling, and incident response. These procedures should be clearly documented and accessible to relevant personnel.
5. **Provide Comprehensive Training and Support:** Equip your team with the necessary knowledge and skills to manage cloud resources effectively. Training programs should cover the specific technologies and platforms being used, as well as best practices for cloud security and operations.

6. **Establish communication channels:** Maintain proactive communication with your cloud service providers. Regular updates, support meetings, and a clear understanding of the service level agreements (SLAs) can help preemptively address potential issues.
7. **Continuously optimize and improve the cloud environment:** Conduct periodic reviews of your cloud setup to identify opportunities for cost savings, performance improvements, or additional security enhancements. Adjust your cloud usage and configurations as your organizational needs evolve and as new cloud features become available.

By adhering to these detailed steps and maintaining a strategic focus on each stage of the cloud journey, organizations can create a dynamic, secure, and efficient cloud environment that aligns with their business goals and provides a foundation for future growth.

CHAPTER 15

Tools and Services

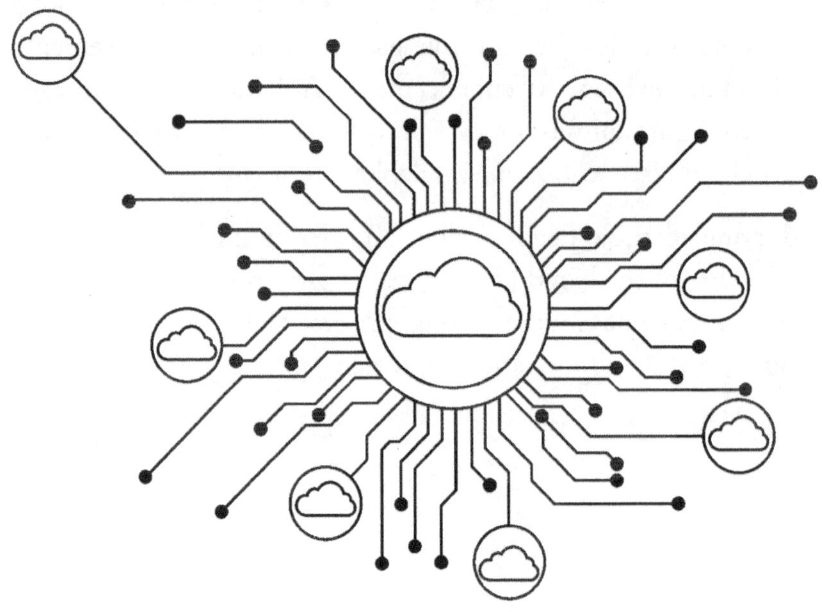

The transition to cloud computing can be facilitated by a range of specialized tools and services designed to streamline the migration process. Below are several categories, each with a brief explanation and instances of associated tools:

1. **Cloud Migration Assessment Tools:** These tools evaluate an organization's current infrastructure and applications to determine how ready they are for moving to the cloud. For example, tools like AWS Migration Hub offer insights into the readiness of different workloads for migration.
2. **Cloud Migration Planning Tools:** Such tools aid in crafting and tracking a comprehensive cloud migration strategy, detailing each step, milestone, and resource allocation. Tools like Trello or

Asana can help teams collaborate on and monitor the progress of migration projects.

3. **Cloud Migration Automation Tools:** With these, repetitive tasks in the migration process are automated, such as data replication and application transfer, ensuring a more efficient and error-free migration. Tools such as Terraform allow for infrastructure as code, automating the provisioning of cloud services.
4. **Cloud Migration Testing Tools:** These are crucial for validating the functionality and performance of applications post-migration. Tools like Selenium can automate testing of web applications in the new cloud environment.
5. **Cloud Migration Monitoring Tools:** Post-migration, these tools keep a continuous check on cloud resources, application performance, and health of the services. Tools like Datadog provide real-time monitoring and alerts for cloud infrastructures.
6. **Cloud Migration Security and Compliance Tools:** To ensure that migrated applications and data adhere to necessary security standards and regulations, these tools provide continuous security assessments and compliance monitoring. For instance, Qualys offers cloud security assessments to identify vulnerabilities and ensure compliance.
7. **Cloud Migration Support Services:** Often provided by cloud vendors or specialized third-party companies, these services range from expert consultancy to hands-on training and technical support to guide organizations through the migration journey. Many cloud providers, including AWS and Microsoft Azure, offer comprehensive professional services to support customers before, during, and after migration.

CHAPTER 16

Licensing and Cost Analysis

Conducting a thorough analysis of licensing needs and costs is a key part of planning for a transition to cloud services. It ensures that an organization can forecast the financial implications of the move and maintain compliance with software usage policies. Below are structured steps to guide you through this process:

Identify licensing requirements:

Pinpoint the necessary software licenses for the applications and services slated for cloud migration. This encompasses licenses for operating systems, databases, middleware, and additional software components.

1. **Identify the applications and software:** Compile a detailed list of all software licenses currently held. This should include operating systems, database licenses, and any application-specific licenses.

2. **Determine the licensing model:** Examine the licensing models available for each piece of software. This could range from traditional perpetual licenses to subscription-based models often used in cloud services.
3. **Review licensing terms and conditions:** Scrutinize the terms and conditions attached to each software license. It's crucial to understand any constraints or limitations that could impact the use of software in a cloud environment.
4. **Consider licensing portability:** Investigate whether current licenses can be transferred to a cloud setting. Some vendors may allow existing licenses to be used in the cloud, often referred to as "bring your own license" (BYOL) policies.
5. **Identify licensing dependencies:** Establish clear links between licenses and their dependent systems. Some applications might need specific versions of databases or middleware that also require licensing considerations.
6. **Evaluate licensing costs:** Compare current on-premise licensing costs with those associated with cloud-based alternatives. This comparison should consider not only direct costs but also potential savings from reduced on-premise hardware and maintenance.

Assess licensing options:

When planning for cloud migration, a thorough assessment of licensing options is essential for both operational and financial strategy. This assessment ensures the organization's licensing strategy is in sync with its cloud adoption goals, which may include scalability, performance enhancements, or cost savings.

Here's how organizations can effectively assess their licensing options:

1. **Identify licensing models:** Document the available licensing arrangements for each software item slated for migration. This includes perpetual on-premise licenses and cloud-based subscriptions.

2. **Compare licensing models:** Understand the different licensing mechanisms on offer. Some applications may allow for direct transfer to the cloud, while others might require new, cloud-specific licenses.
3. **Evaluate licensing terms and conditions:** Determine whether existing on-premise licenses can be moved to the cloud environment, a concept known as "bring your own license" (BYOL), which could lead to cost reductions.
4. **Review vendor policies:** Investigate the licensing options available through cloud providers' marketplaces, as these may offer financial advantages through discounts or bundled services.
5. **Assess cost-effectiveness:** Carry out a detailed comparison of current licensing expenditures against those projected for the cloud, considering future scalability that could impact licensing needs.
6. **Consider scalability:** Evaluate the scalability and adaptability of each licensing alternative. Certain cloud licensing models may provide enhanced scalability, an important factor for organizations anticipating growth or variable demand.
7. **Analyze vendor support:** Consider the level of support each licensing model entails. This includes the availability of technical assistance, regular updates, and the handling of maintenance duties..

Estimate infrastructure costs:

Calculate the infrastructure expenses related to cloud transition, factoring in the costs for computational resources, data storage, and network bandwidth. Employ cloud cost estimation tools or calculators to gauge these expenses.

1. **Identify compute resources:** Begin by assessing the required compute resources for each application or workload scheduled for cloud migration. This includes the needs for virtual machines, containers, and serverless computing resources.

2. **Determine storage requirements:** Evaluate the storage demands of each application or workload. This may include a variety of storage types such as block, file, or object storage solutions offered by cloud providers.
3. **Evaluate network bandwidth requirements:** Assess the bandwidth needs crucial for the transfer and operation of applications in the cloud. Take into account all data movement including incoming, outgoing, and data transfers between different cloud regions or services.
4. **Consider backup and disaster recovery:** Factor in the cost implications for backing up data and establishing disaster recovery protocols. Consider the pricing for additional storage and the data transfer rates for these activities.
5. **Estimate infrastructure costs:** Utilize tools provided by cloud service providers, such as AWS Pricing Calculator or Azure Pricing Calculator, to estimate the costs based on the identified compute, storage, and bandwidth needs.
6. **Optimize infrastructure costs:** Finally, explore ways to optimize these costs. For instance, committing to reserved instances for a term could lower compute costs, while data transfer services might offer cost savings on bandwidth utilization.

Estimate data transfer costs:

Determine the expenses related to moving data into and out of the cloud environment. This includes the costs for both incoming and outgoing data transfers, as well as transfers between different regions or zones within the cloud.

To accurately forecast the expenses related to data movement during cloud migration, consider the following steps:

1. **Identify data transfer requirements:** Initially, pinpoint the data movement needs for each application or workload being

transitioned to the cloud. This analysis should encompass all data traffic directions, including inbound, outbound, and within or between different cloud regions or zones.

2. **Determine data transfer volume:** Calculate the volume of data that will be shifted to and from the cloud. This estimation is typically based on the size of the data sets, databases, or other relevant data containers scheduled for migration.
3. **Evaluate data transfer options:** Investigate various methods available for transferring data to the cloud. This may include services that accelerate data transfer or dedicated connectivity solutions. Assess each method's cost-effectiveness and efficiency to select the best option.
4. **Data Transfer Cost Estimation:** Utilize tools such as the AWS Pricing Calculator or similar resources from other cloud providers to estimate the costs associated with the data transfer, based on the identified volume and the selected transfer method.
5. **Optimize data transfer costs:** Explore ways to minimize data transfer costs. Techniques could include compressing data to reduce its size or using specialized services that expedite data transfer at lower costs.

Consider operational costs:

Consider the costs involved in overseeing the cloud environment. This includes expenditures for monitoring, support, and administrative tasks.

To accurately evaluate the operational costs of cloud migration, undertake the following steps:

1. **Identify operational requirements:** Begin by determining the operational needs for each application or workload migrating to the cloud. This includes routine management and maintenance duties, such as monitoring application

performance, ensuring security measures, and adhering to compliance regulations.

2. **Determine staffing requirements:** Assess the staffing needs for managing the cloud infrastructure. This involves determining the number and expertise of administrators, engineers, and other support staff necessary to maintain and support the cloud operations effectively.
3. **Evaluate training needs:** Evaluate the training requirements for your current workforce to ensure they possess or can develop the skills and knowledge needed to manage cloud operations efficiently. This might include training in cloud technologies, security protocols, or specific cloud management tools.
4. **Operational Costs Estimation:** Utilize cloud cost calculators or similar estimation tools to gauge the operational costs. These should be based on the identified staffing, training needs, and other operational factors.
5. **Optimize operational costs:** Explore ways to streamline operational costs. This could involve automating routine tasks to reduce manual labor or considering third-party managed services, which might offer cost-effective solutions compared to in-house management, particularly for specialized tasks or round-the-clock monitoring.

Compare costs:

Evaluate the projected expenses of on-premise infrastructure against those of cloud-based deployment. Take into account the upfront and recurring costs linked to each choice.

For a thorough cost comparison in the context of cloud migration, proceed with these steps:

1. **Identify the Cost Categories:** Start by categorizing the expenses related to cloud migration. Common categories

include infrastructure expenses, software licensing, data transfer fees, and the costs of ongoing operations.

2. **Evaluate on-premise costs:** Review the existing on-premise costs for each category. This step usually involves a thorough examination of bills, contracts, and other financial documents to get a clear picture of current expenditures.
3. **Estimate Cloud Costs:** Utilize cloud cost calculators or similar tools to estimate the expenses for each category within a cloud environment. This estimation should include considerations for compute power, storage needs, network bandwidth, data transfer volumes, and operational requirements specific to the cloud.
4. **Detailed Cost Comparison:** Lay out the estimated cloud costs alongside the current on-premise costs for a detailed comparison. This comparison should highlight areas of potential savings or any additional costs that cloud migration might incur.
5. **Consider other factors:** Go beyond mere financial numbers and consider other qualitative factors that might influence costs. This includes the potential for enhanced agility, scalability options, and opportunities for innovation that cloud environments typically offer.
6. **Conduct a Cost-Benefit Analysis:** Develop an analysis that weighs both the tangible costs and intangible benefits of migrating to the cloud. Such an analysis will provide a broader perspective on the financial viability and strategic advantages of cloud migration.

Optimize costs:

Seek ways to reduce costs, like utilizing reserved instances, spot instances, or embracing serverless computing services to cut down on infrastructure expenses.

To optimize costs for cloud migration, follow these steps:

1. **Continuously monitor usage:** Establish a system for continuous monitoring of cloud resources usage, including compute power, storage, and network bandwidth. Regular monitoring helps in identifying underused resources, enabling their optimization or decommissioning, which can lead to cost savings.
2. **Implement Automation Tools:** Deploy automation tools for managing the cloud environment. Automation can significantly reduce the time and manual effort involved in maintenance and management, leading to lower operational costs.
3. **Utilize Reserved Instances:** Take advantage of reserved instances or similar long-term usage pricing models offered by cloud providers. These models often come with discounted rates, reducing infrastructure costs and providing more predictable budgeting.
4. **Consider spot instances:** For flexible or non-critical workloads, consider using spot instances. While they offer substantial cost savings, they do come with the possibility of interruptions, so they're best suited for tasks that can withstand sudden stops.
5. **Optimize Data Transfer:** Implement strategies to minimize data transfer costs. This can include compressing data, using data transfer acceleration services, and leveraging edge caching services to decrease the volume of data being transferred.
6. **Leverage managed services:** Utilize managed services provided by cloud providers or third-party vendors. These services can encompass areas such as database management, security, and monitoring, and can reduce the burden and cost of managing these aspects in-house.

CHAPTER 17

OPEX (Ongoing Operational Expenses) Licensing & Other Commercials

Ongoing Operational Expenses (OPEX) in cloud migration include licensing fees and various business-related expenses. Examples of OPEX in cloud migration, such as licensing and commercial expenses, are:

Ongoing Operational Expenses (OPEX) for Cloud Migration	Description
Subscription Fees	Ongoing subscription fees for cloud services, such as compute, storage, and networking resources.
Usage Fees	Usage-based fees for cloud services, such as data transfer or API calls.

License Fees	Ongoing license fees for software or applications running in the cloud environment.
Support and Maintenance Fees	Ongoing support and maintenance fees for software, applications, or cloud services.
Training and Certification Costs	Ongoing costs for training and certification of staff to manage and maintain the cloud environment.
Security and Compliance Costs	Ongoing costs for security and compliance measures, such as data encryption, access controls, and regulatory compliance.
Backup and Disaster Recovery Costs	Ongoing costs for backup and disaster recovery solutions to ensure business continuity in the event of a data loss or system failure.
Consulting and Professional Services Costs	Ongoing costs for consulting and professional services to assist with cloud migration,optimization, and management.

The table above outlines various continuous operational expenses (OPEX) associated with cloud migration. It includes items such as subscription charges, usage fees, licensing costs, support and maintenance expenses, expenses for training and certifications, costs related to security and compliance, charges for backup and disaster recovery, as well as fees for consulting and professional services. Factoring in these costs is crucial for organizations to accurately budget and prepare for the ongoing financial implications of cloud migration.

CHAPTER 18

Define Policies and How to Implement Them

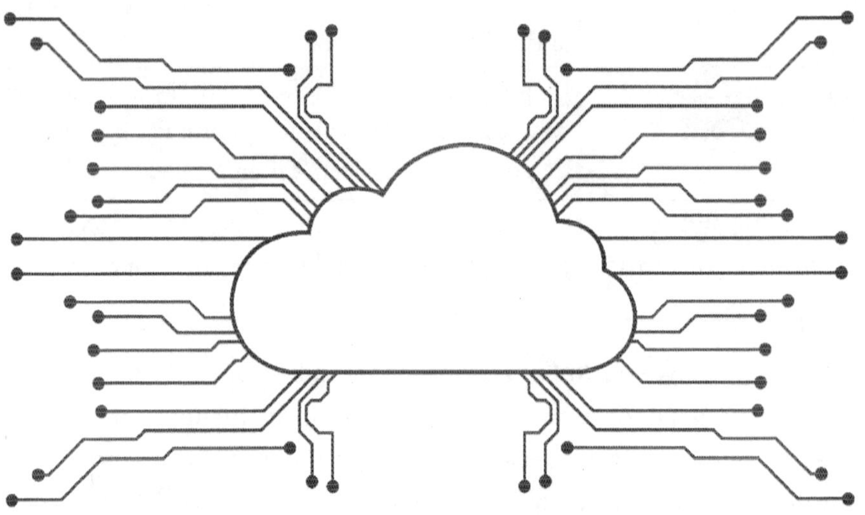

Cloud policies are essential for organizations utilizing cloud computing, serving as a comprehensive set of guidelines to ensure the appropriate and effective use of cloud resources. These policies encompass various areas crucial for maintaining operational integrity and aligning with both business and technical requirements, while also adhering to necessary governance and compliance standards.

Key elements of cloud policies include data security and privacy, which are fundamental in industries like healthcare, where protecting patient data is crucial for HIPAA compliance. Access controls form another vital aspect, determining who can access specific cloud resources, a factor especially pertinent in sectors like finance where data sensitivity is high.

Service level agreements outlined in cloud policies set clear performance expectations and responses in cases of non-compliance, much like a retail business would require robust data encryption and secure transaction processing in its cloud usage. Compliance requirements are integral, ensuring that organizations adhere to various regulatory standards, which are essential for lawful operations.

Incident response guidelines are also a significant part of cloud policies, providing a structured approach to handle issues like security violations. This includes immediate actions and long-term strategies to mitigate impacts, such as in an IT firm where rapid response to data breaches is critical.

The policies also guide the selection and management of cloud service providers, ensuring that the providers align with the organization's specific needs, whether it's for security, cost-efficiency, or service quality. Finally, they dictate how resources within the cloud should be allocated and managed, which is vital for maintaining efficiency and cost-effectiveness in any cloud-dependent operation.

Here are some of the key cloud policies to consider:

1. **Data Security and Privacy Policies:** Critical for protecting data within the cloud, they specify encryption standards, data access control mechanisms, and adherence to data privacy regulations to safeguard sensitive information.
2. **Access Control Policies:** Essential for defining authorization levels, delineating who can access specific cloud resources and the nature of permitted interactions, thus preventing unauthorized access and ensuring data integrity.
3. **Service Level Agreements (SLAs):** Agreements that outline the expected service standards from cloud providers. They should cover aspects like system uptime, promptness in response, and efficiency in resolving issues, ensuring reliability and accountability.

4. **Compliance Policies:** Designed to ensure the organization's cloud usage complies with relevant regulations. Especially important for adherence to standards like HIPAA in healthcare, GDPR for data protection in Europe, and SOX for financial practices.
5. **Incident Response Policies:** Set out the procedures for managing security incidents or operational disruptions. Vital for quick response and resolution, minimizing the impact of such incidents.
6. **Cloud Provider Selection Policies:** Outline the criteria for selecting cloud service providers. Factors such as security measures, performance metrics, and cost efficiency are crucial for making informed decisions.
7. **Cloud Provider Management Policies:** Aimed at managing relationships with cloud service providers, they should cover ongoing monitoring, performance reporting, and effective resolution of issues to maintain service quality.
8. **Cloud Resource Allocation Policies:** Govern the allocation and management of cloud resources. They focus on efficient cost distribution, optimizing resource utilization, and strategic capacity planning to align with the organization's operational needs.

Understanding the implementation of policies is crucial, as these policies are crafted to align cloud usage with business and technical needs while adhering to governance and compliance standards. Failing to effectively implement these policies can leave an organization vulnerable to data loss, security breaches, and non-compliance issues.

Implementing cloud policies effectively is a multi-faceted process, essential for enhancing cloud security, minimizing risks, and harnessing the full potential of cloud resources. Here's how organizations can implement these policies:

1. **Define policies:** Create comprehensive policies governing cloud usage. These should encompass data security, access control, adherence to service level agreements, and compliance with legal standards. For instance, a company like Salesforce might develop robust data security policies to protect their vast customer data in the cloud.
2. **Communicate policies:** Clearly convey these policies to everyone involved in cloud operations, from IT personnel and business users to external vendors. The objective is to ensure complete understanding and alignment with the organization's goals. A good example here is how IBM regularly updates and communicates its cloud policies to all stakeholders to ensure everyone is on the same page.
3. **Monitor compliance:** Regularly check adherence to these policies through audits, reviews, and evaluations. Google, for example, conducts routine audits to ensure compliance with its cloud security policies.
4. **Enforce policies:** In cases of policy violations, implement corrective measures such as access restriction, incident reporting to management, or vendor contract termination. Amazon Web Services (AWS), for example, has a strict policy enforcement regime that includes immediate actions against non-compliance.
5. **Continuously improve policies:** Constantly refine policies based on stakeholder feedback, evolving regulatory landscapes, and changing business or technical needs. Microsoft Azure, for example, continuously updates its cloud policies to adapt to new regulatory requirements and technological advancements.

CHAPTER 19

Landing Zone Assessment

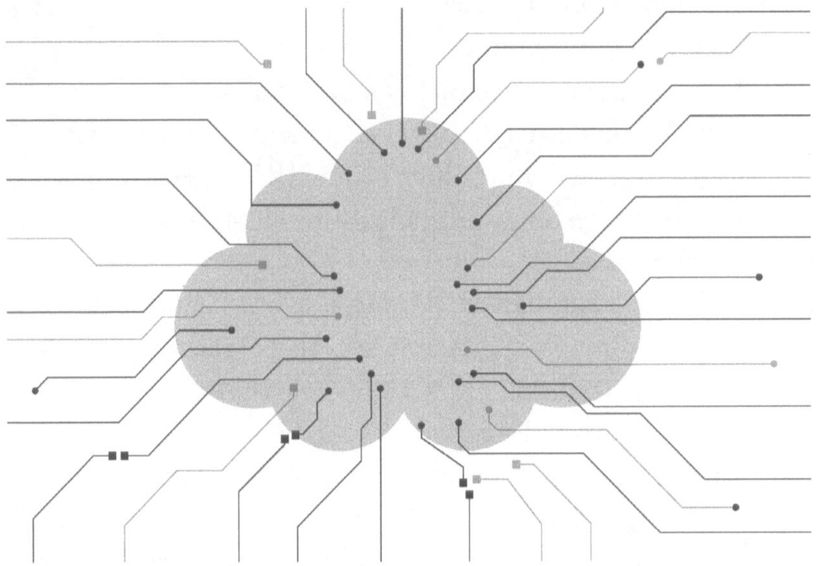

A Landing Zone Assessment is an essential step for organizations preparing for cloud migration. This process thoroughly examines the existing IT infrastructure, spotlighting areas such as application setup, network structure, security measures, compliance adherence, and overall business aims.

The purpose of this assessment is to pinpoint potential hurdles in transitioning to cloud platforms. It is instrumental in devising a migration strategy that ensures secure, compliant, and efficient transfer of workloads to the cloud. This tailored approach caters to the specific demands and challenges unique to each organization.

Conducting a Landing Zone Assessment typically involves a team of specialists with deep expertise in cloud architecture, security, compliance, and migration strategies. The assessment is often a blend of methodologies, including stakeholder interviews, review of existing documentation, and technical evaluations of the current IT landscape.

The outcome of a Landing Zone Assessment is a comprehensive report that delineates an organization's readiness for cloud migration. This report plays a pivotal role in identifying any potential obstacles or risks associated with the transition to a cloud environment. More importantly, it provides actionable strategies to overcome these challenges. This document essentially acts as a navigational guide for the entire migration journey, laying the groundwork for a meticulously crafted migration strategy.

The significance of a Landing Zone Assessment lies in its capacity to prepare an organization's infrastructure for a smooth transition to cloud services. Through this assessment, organizations can uncover and address any potential hindrances or risks linked to cloud migration. This preemptive approach is crucial in mitigating migration-related risks, thus paving the way for a successful and efficient shift to cloud-based solutions.

The significance of conducting a Landing Zone Assessment during cloud migration can be highlighted through four key points:

1. **Assessment of Migration Readiness:** The primary purpose of a Landing Zone Assessment is to gauge an organization's preparedness for migrating to a cloud environment. It involves a thorough examination of the existing IT infrastructure, assessing various elements like applications, network structure, security status, and adherence to compliance norms. This step is crucial in ensuring that the organization's IT landscape is adequately aligned for a seamless migration.
2. **Identification of Potential Hurdles:** One of the pivotal outcomes of this assessment is the identification of potential obstacles or risks that might obstruct the cloud migration process. These could range from technical difficulties and

security or compliance concerns to limitations posed by existing budgets. Recognizing these challenges beforehand is crucial in strategizing effective solutions and mitigating risks.

3. **Develop a plan:** Based on the insights gained from the assessment, a Landing Zone Assessment culminates in the creation of a strategic plan for cloud migration. This plan acts as a comprehensive guide, outlining steps to overcome the identified roadblocks and ensuring a well-orchestrated transition to the cloud. This planning phase is fundamental to orchestrating a migration process that is efficient, secure, and aligned with organizational objectives.
4. **Optimization of Cloud Resources:** Beyond merely facilitating migration, a Landing Zone Assessment can also uncover opportunities for more efficient utilization of cloud resources. This aspect of the assessment focuses on areas where improvements can be made, such as cost reduction, enhancing system performance, or bolstering security measures. This ensures that the move to the cloud not only aligns with operational needs but also optimizes resource usage for better overall outcomes.

PHASE 4

MIGRATION PHASE

CHAPTER 20

Migration Overview

The migration phase in cloud migration is critical for several key reasons:

1. **Minimizes Downtime:** A major aspect of the migration phase is the transfer of applications and data from an organization's existing on-premises setup to a cloud-based infrastructure. This transition, while necessary, can be quite extensive and may lead to downtime. Such downtime, even if brief, can potentially disrupt an organization's operations. Therefore, meticulous planning and efficient execution during the migration phase are imperative to reduce downtime as much as possible, thereby maintaining uninterrupted business operations.

2. **Ensures Data Integrity:** During the migration phase, the integrity of the data being transferred is paramount. This includes ensuring the accuracy, consistency, and completeness of data as it moves from the on-premises infrastructure to the cloud. It's crucial to have mechanisms in place to verify that the data remains intact and reliable throughout this process. This might involve implementing data validation checks, ensuring data formatting is preserved, and confirming that no data is lost or corrupted during the transfer.
3. **Mitigates Security Risks:** One of the critical aspects of the migration phase is the secure transfer of sensitive data and applications to the cloud. This phase demands robust security measures to protect this data during the transfer process. Employing strong encryption methods and stringent access control mechanisms is vital to safeguarding the data against potential breaches or unauthorized access.
4. **Optimizes Infrastructure:** The migration phase also presents an opportunity for organizations to reassess and refine their IT infrastructure. This process involves a thorough evaluation of existing applications, workloads, and data storage setups. Through this assessment, organizations can identify areas of inefficiency or redundancy within their current systems. Such insights enable them to restructure and optimize their cloud infrastructure, leading to cost reductions and enhanced performance.
5. **Enables Compliance:** Another crucial aspect of the migration phase is the alignment of the cloud infrastructure with relevant legal and regulatory standards. This step involves a detailed review of compliance requirements related to data privacy, security, and specific industry regulations. By addressing any compliance gaps during the migration, organizations can ensure their cloud operations adhere to necessary legal frameworks.

CHAPTER 21

Migrate Lift and Shift

The lift and shift migration phase, also known as rehosting, involves transferring an existing application along with its associated infrastructure directly to a cloud environment with minimal alterations. This strategy focuses on moving the application's code, data, and dependencies to the cloud in their existing form.

Often chosen as an initial step in broader cloud migration strategies, lift and shift is valued for its relative speed, simplicity, and cost-effectiveness. It enables organizations to transition their applications to the cloud without needing extensive changes to their underlying code or architecture. This method is particularly advantageous for complex applications that are challenging to modify or redesign.

However, a key consideration with lift and shift migration is that it might not fully leverage the potential benefits offered by cloud computing.

Applications moved in this manner may not be inherently optimized for cloud environments, potentially leading to missed opportunities in terms of scalability, flexibility, and cost efficiency inherent in cloud services.

To address this, organizations often engage in a subsequent phase of cloud optimization. In this phase, the application and its infrastructure undergo further examination and refinement to better suit the cloud environment. This might involve architectural adjustments, optimization for cloud-specific features, and implementing industry-standard practices for cloud security and management. Through these refinements, organizations aim to enhance application performance, scalability, and reliability while also realizing cost savings and operational efficiencies.

Ultimately, the lift and shift migration phase serve as a foundational step in transitioning to cloud computing. It allows organizations to quickly and cost-effectively migrate their applications to the cloud. To maximize the benefits of the cloud, it is crucial to engage in further optimization post-migration, ensuring that applications are not just hosted in the cloud but are fully adapted to and integrated with the cloud's unique capabilities and advantages.

CHAPTER 22

Migrate Simplex Data and Apps

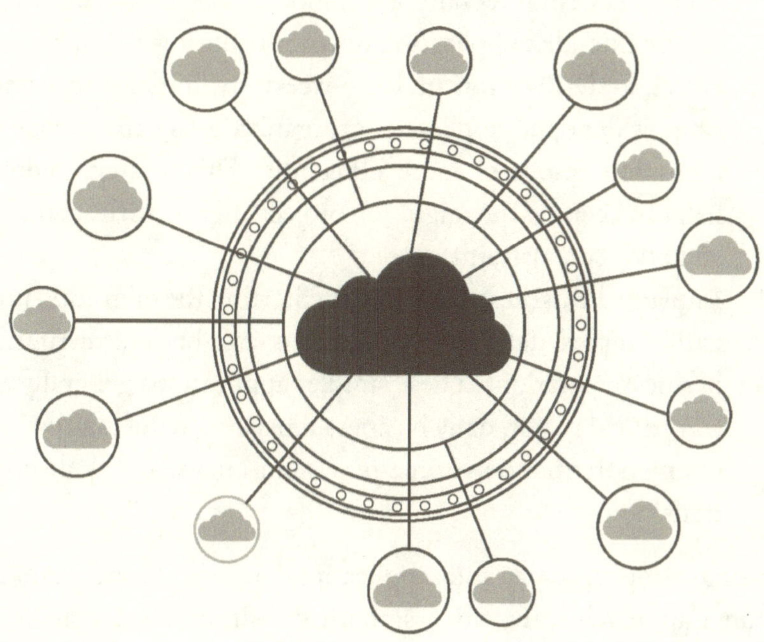

Migrating simplex data and applications, which are characterized by their straightforward architecture, minimal dependencies, and limited integrations, is often less complicated than dealing with complex data and applications. This migration involves shifting these simple data and applications to cloud infrastructure with little to no modification in their structure or coding.

The approach of prioritizing simplex data and applications for cloud migration is significant for several reasons:

1. **Faster Time to Value:** Moving simplex data and applications to the cloud can be accomplished more rapidly compared to

complex counterparts. This expedites the process, allowing organizations to benefit from cloud computing's advantages sooner, thereby achieving a quicker return on their cloud investment.

2. **Reduced Risk:** The straightforward nature of simplex data and applications, characterized by their fewer interdependencies and simpler system integrations, minimizes the risk factors like data loss or extended application downtime during the migration.
3. **Efficient Utilization of Resources:** By initially focusing on simpler data and applications, organizations can manage their migration resources more efficiently. This strategic approach helps in keeping the migration project aligned with set timelines and budget constraints.
4. **Improved Business Continuity:** Starting the migration process with simplex data and applications can be less disruptive to business operations. These simpler applications generally play a less critical role in daily business functions, reducing the impact of any potential downtime or system unavailability during the transition.

Migrating simplex data and applications to the cloud requires a structured approach to ensure a smooth transition. Here are the steps organizations should take:

1. **Initial Assessment of Data and Applications:** Begin by evaluating the simplex data and applications earmarked for cloud migration. This involves scrutinizing their architecture, understanding the dependencies they have, and examining how they integrate with other systems. For instance, applications with minimal external dependencies are typically easier to migrate.
2. **Selecting an Appropriate Migration Strategy:** After assessment, decide on the best migration method for these simpler systems. This decision could range from a straightforward 'lift and shift' approach, which involves moving applications

without modification, to more complex strategies like re-platforming (modifying applications to better suit the cloud) or containerization (encapsulating applications in containers for easier portability).

3. **Developing a Migration Plan:** Construct a detailed migration roadmap. This should include a timeline for the migration, identify any interdependencies, and highlight potential risks and how to mitigate them. A well-crafted plan will serve as a blueprint for the migration process.
4. **Conducting Migration Tests:** Before fully committing to migrating everything, it's prudent to perform a trial run. Testing the migration with a small segment of data or a less critical application can reveal unforeseen challenges or necessary adjustments, reducing the risk of major issues during the full-scale migration.
5. **Executing the Migration:** With successful testing, proceed to migrate the identified simplex data and applications. This phase should be closely monitored to ensure adherence to the migration plan and to quickly resolve any issues that may arise during the transition.

In the process of migrating simplex data and applications to the cloud, there are several vital factors that organizations need to consider to ensure that the migration is successful and beneficial. These key considerations include:

1. **Application and Data Compatibility:** One of the first steps is to verify that the applications and data are compatible with the chosen cloud infrastructure. This involves checking if they can operate effectively in the cloud environment and meeting all the specific requirements set by the cloud provider.
2. **Security and Compliance:** Security is paramount in cloud migrations. It's crucial to implement robust security measures, like data encryption and strict access controls, to safeguard applications and data during and after the migration.

Additionally, compliance with relevant industry standards and regulations must be upheld to avoid legal and reputational risks.

3. **Cost Assessment:** A thorough cost analysis is essential. This encompasses estimating not just the immediate costs of the cloud infrastructure and the migration process, but also long-term expenses related to maintenance, support, and any potential scaling.
4. **Developing a Clear Migration Strategy:** A well-defined migration strategy should be in place, detailing each step of the process, the timelines involved, dependencies between different applications or data sets, and addressing potential risks. This strategy should also determine the most suitable migration method and include a provision for testing the migration on a smaller scale before full deployment.
5. **Data Backup and Recovery:** Ensuring the availability of a reliable backup and recovery strategy is crucial, especially in the context of data migration. This means having backups ready before starting the migration and testing recovery procedures to guarantee data integrity and availability post-migration.
6. **Monitoring and Optimization:** Once the migration is complete, it's important to not just leave the applications and data as they are. Continuous monitoring for performance, scalability, and cost-effectiveness is necessary. This could involve regular checks and tweaks to ensure that the cloud resources are being utilized optimally and cost-efficiently.

CHAPTER 23

Migrate Complex Apps and Databases

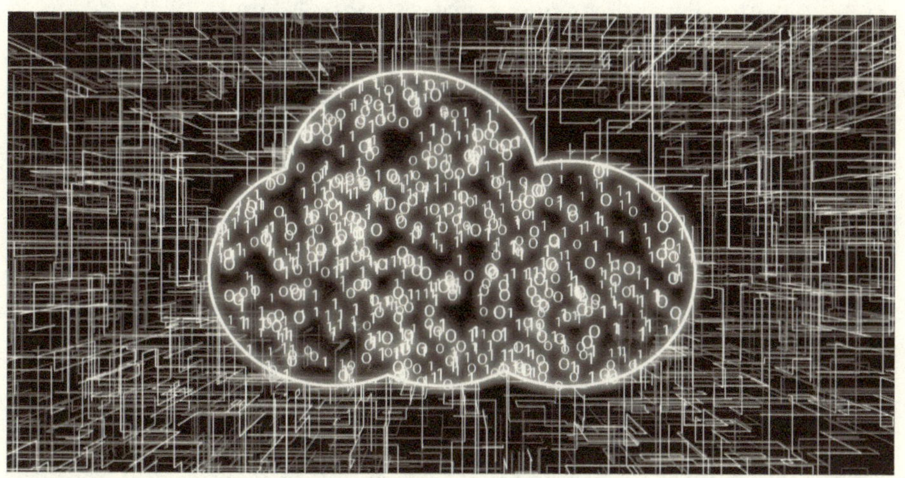

Migrating complex applications and databases to a cloud environment demands a nuanced and thorough approach, given their intricate architectures, myriad dependencies, and extensive integration with other systems. To navigate this complex migration effectively, organizations need to focus on several key aspects:

1. **Application and Database Architecture:** A deep dive into the architecture of applications and databases is crucial. This involves pinpointing any dependencies, integrations, or custom features that might influence the migration. Special attention should be paid to legacy systems or outdated software that may not easily align with modern cloud infrastructures.
2. **Data Migration:** When it comes to complex applications, data migration is often a cornerstone of the process. Migrating substantial volumes of data from traditional data centers to the cloud requires a robust plan, encompassing data validation,

thorough data cleansing, and meticulous data mapping. This ensures the data's accuracy and integrity in its new cloud environment.

3. **Security and Compliance:** The security and compliance of applications and databases during migration cannot be overstated. Critical security measures, such as robust encryption protocols and stringent access controls, must be in place to safeguard sensitive data throughout the transition. Additionally, compliance with relevant regulations and standards must be diligently maintained.
4. **Migration Strategy:** A detailed and well-structured migration strategy is vital. This strategy should clearly outline every phase of the migration, including schedules, dependencies, and potential risks. Selecting the most suitable migration approach and conducting comprehensive pre-migration testing are integral parts of this process.
5. **Performance and Optimization Post-Migration:** Once migration is complete, it's essential to continually monitor and fine-tune the application and database performance. This continuous oversight ensures that they are functioning optimally, efficiently using resources, and providing the desired scalability and cost-effectiveness.
6. **Disaster Recovery and Business Continuity:** A comprehensive disaster recovery strategy is critical, particularly for complex applications and databases. Ensuring that these systems can be quickly and effectively restored in the event of data loss or system failure is paramount for maintaining business continuity.

Migrating complex applications and databases to a cloud setting involves a series of strategic steps, each crucial for ensuring a successful transition:

1. **Evaluate the Existing Environment:** Begin by thoroughly evaluating the current setup of applications and databases. This step is essential for identifying any dependencies, integrations,

and customizations that could influence the migration process. Attention should be given to older legacy systems or software that might not align with cloud technologies.

2. **Selecting the Appropriate Migration Approach:** It's crucial to choose a migration method tailored to the complexity of the application and database. Options include 'lift and shift,' re-platforming, or refactoring. Each approach has its pros and cons, so it's important to select one that aligns closely with the organization's specific needs.
3. **Develop a Migration Plan:** Develop a detailed plan that outlines the migration timeline, acknowledges dependencies, and anticipates potential risks. This strategy should encompass selecting a migration method, implementing a robust testing protocol, and crafting a data migration plan.
4. **Executing Data Migration:** Given the intricacies of complex applications, the data migration process is paramount. A well-thought-out data migration plan should include steps for validating, cleansing, and mapping the data to ensure accuracy and integrity in the cloud.
5. **Testing and Optimization Post-Migration:** Once the migration is complete, it's essential to rigorously test the applications and databases in their new cloud environment. Performance, load, and scalability tests are critical at this stage. Continuous monitoring and optimization post-migration are also crucial to maintain optimal performance, scalability, and cost-effectiveness.
6. **Ensuring Disaster Recovery and Business Continuity:** Developing a solid disaster recovery plan is non-negotiable. It's vital to ensure that the complex applications and databases can be swiftly restored in case of system failure or data loss.
7. **Security and Compliance:** Security and compliance are top priorities during migration. It's important to migrate applications and databases securely, adhering to relevant

standards and regulations. Implementing robust security measures, including encryption and access control, is key to protecting data and applications throughout the migration process.

What are the crucial factors to consider in this process?

When transitioning complex applications and databases to the cloud, several critical factors must be thoroughly considered to ensure a seamless and successful migration:

1. **Evaluating Application and Database Architecture:** A foundational step is to carefully examine the existing architecture of applications and databases. This evaluation helps identify any dependencies, integrations, or specific customizations that might influence the migration process. Particular attention should be paid to older systems or software that may not readily adapt to cloud environments.
2. **Executing a Detailed Data Migration Plan:** Moving extensive volumes of data to a cloud infrastructure is a pivotal aspect of migrating complex applications. To manage this effectively, it's crucial to devise a comprehensive data migration strategy. This plan should encompass thorough data validation, cleansing, and mapping processes to guarantee the precise and accurate transfer of data to the cloud.
3. **Prioritizing Security and Compliance:** Ensuring the security of applications and databases during migration is paramount. Organizations must adhere to relevant standards and regulations. Implementing robust security measures, including data encryption and stringent access controls, is vital for safeguarding data throughout the migration journey.
4. **Strategizing the Migration:** Developing a detailed and well-thought-out migration strategy is key. This strategy should clearly outline the entire migration process, establish timelines, recognize dependencies, and anticipate potential challenges

or risks. Selecting an appropriate migration method tailored to the organization's needs and conducting comprehensive testing before the full-scale migration are crucial steps in this strategy.

5. **Performance and Optimization:** Post-migration, it's crucial to regularly monitor and fine-tune the applications and databases now in the cloud. This ongoing process ensures they perform optimally, scale efficiently, and remain cost-effective. Regular performance analysis can identify areas for improvement, like optimizing database queries or scaling resources during peak usage times.
6. **Disaster Recovery and Business Continuity:** Developing a robust disaster recovery plan is essential. Organizations need to ensure that in the event of a system failure or data loss, there are mechanisms in place for quick recovery. This might involve implementing cloud-based backup solutions and having clear procedures for data restoration and system failover.
7. **Cost:** Migrating complex systems to the cloud can be an expensive endeavor. It's vital to carefully estimate and plan for the costs involved, including the expenses for cloud infrastructure, the migration process itself, and ongoing maintenance and support. Tools like AWS Cost Explorer or Azure Cost Management can aid in forecasting and managing these expenses.
8. **Skillset and Resources:** Complex migrations often require specialized skills and resources. Organizations should evaluate their internal capabilities and consider whether additional training or hiring is necessary. For instance, migrating a large-scale database might require expertise in cloud-based database technologies, which existing staff may not possess. In such cases, seeking external expertise or investing in training for internal teams can be beneficial.

PHASE 5

CLOUD OPERATE PHASE

CHAPTER 24

Cloud Operationalization

The Cloud Operate phase marks the concluding stage of the cloud migration journey, where organizations fully engage with their newly established cloud environment for operational activities. This phase is crucial, as it involves the practical, day-to-day usage of the cloud to run applications and manage data. Here are the key activities involved in the Cloud Operate phase:

1. **Application and Data Monitoring:** In this phase, it's vital to keep a vigilant eye on the performance and functionality of applications and data. Continuous monitoring helps in quickly identifying and resolving any operational issues. Utilizing cloud monitoring tools like Amazon CloudWatch or Google Cloud Monitoring can provide insights into application performance, helping to maintain optimal operations.
2. **Continuous Optimization:** A proactive approach to tweaking and refining the cloud setup ensures optimal performance and cost-efficiency. This might involve reconfiguring the storage solutions, fine-tuning network bandwidth usage,

or adjusting compute resources to match the fluctuating demands better.

3. **Security and Compliance:** Keeping the cloud environment secure and in line with regulatory standards is a continual process. It involves implementing robust security measures such as data encryption and strict access control. Regular security audits and compliance checks can help in maintaining a secure cloud infrastructure.
4. **Cost Management:** Monitoring and managing the costs associated with the cloud infrastructure is critical to avoid budget overruns. Tools like AWS Cost Explorer or Azure Cost Management can be instrumental in tracking expenses, allowing for timely identification and correction of any cost-related inefficiencies.
5. **Support and Maintenance:** Ensuring that the cloud environment receives adequate support and maintenance is essential for smooth operations. This includes promptly addressing technical issues, applying necessary updates and patches, and performing routine maintenance tasks to avoid potential disruptions.

CHAPTER 25

New Operating Model

The transition to a cloud environment often leads to substantial shifts in an organization's operating model. This new model is shaped by the organization's strategic objectives, the specificities of their chosen cloud infrastructure, and their overarching business needs. Here are some potential transformations in the operating model post-cloud migration:

1. **Focus on Agility:** Embracing the cloud opens doors to greater organizational agility. The revised operating model might prioritize accelerated development cycles and more regular software updates. This agility allows organizations to swiftly adapt to market shifts and evolving customer demands.
2. **Shift to DevOps:** Migrating to the cloud often paves the way for adopting a DevOps culture. This approach fosters tight integration between development and operations teams, promoting faster, more efficient software development and deployment processes.

3. **Elevated Automation:** In the post-migration landscape, automating routine processes becomes more prominent. This can include automated configurations and resource provisioning, aiming to achieve quicker and more uniform deployment processes.
4. **Centralized Management:** Cloud migration can centralize IT management, streamlining the administration of IT resources. This centralization can lead to more effective resource management and potentially lower operational complexities.
5. **New Skillsets:** Transitioning to cloud computing may necessitate new skills within the workforce. Skills related to cloud management, automation techniques, and enhanced security protocols become crucial. The organization may focus on training existing employees or recruiting new talent with these specialized skills.
6. **Optimizing Costs:** Shifting to the cloud often means moving from a capital expenditure (CapEx) to an operational expenditure (OpEx) model. This transition calls for more adaptable and scalable cost management strategies, with a focus on usage-based pricing models, which can lead to more efficient resource allocation and cost savings.

Preparing for a new operating model post-cloud migration is a multi-step process that enables organizations to fully capitalize on the benefits of cloud computing. Here are the steps organizations can take to effectively plan for this transition:

1. **Define Business Goals:** Begin by clearly defining the business objectives for the new operating model. This involves pinpointing goals like enhanced agility, increased efficiency, or cost reduction, and ensuring the new model is in harmony with these objectives.
2. **Identify Skill Gaps:** Examine the current skill levels within the organization and pinpoint areas where additional expertise is

needed. This step focuses on skills essential for managing cloud infrastructure and those necessary for DevOps implementation.

3. **Create a Comprehensive Training Strategy:** Formulate a plan to develop the required skills, either by training existing staff or recruiting new talent. This should include identifying relevant training programs and certifications that are in line with the demands of the new operational framework.
4. **Assess Current Processes:** Evaluate existing IT processes to identify areas ripe for improvement or adaptation. This often involves integrating automation to streamline operations and cut down on expenses.
5. **Define Governance Policies:** Develop governance policies that align with the new operational model. This includes creating rules and procedures for cloud management, ensuring security and compliance, and efficiently handling data management.
6. **Conduct a Proof of Concept:** Before a full-scale implementation, conduct a smaller, controlled proof of concept. Select a subset of applications or services for initial cloud migration and use this as a test case to evaluate the efficacy of the new operating model.
7. **Develop a Migration Plan:** Put together a thorough plan for the migration process. This plan should cover all phases of migration, including timelines, dependencies, and possible risks, and outline the most suitable migration approach. It's important to thoroughly test the migration strategy before rolling it out across the organization.

CHAPTER 26

New Support Model

Crafting an effective support model post-cloud migration is vital for ensuring that the organization's IT environment aligns with its evolving needs. The model must be adaptable, scalable, and in sync with the organization's core objectives.

Key elements to consider when developing this model are:

1. **Alignment with Business Objectives:** The support framework must be in tune with the organization's strategic objectives. This necessitates establishing well-defined service level agreements (SLAs) and support protocols, guaranteeing that IT resources are leveraged in a manner that furthers these goals.
2. **Scalability and Flexibility:** The support model must have the capacity to adjust to shifts in business demands and expansion within the IT landscape. It should provide a sufficient level of support and be flexible to evolve with changing business requirements. This involves regular assessments and adjustments to the model to ensure it remains effective and efficient.
3. **Multi-Cloud Support:** In an era where multi-cloud strategies are becoming the norm, the support model must be equipped to handle such environments. As organizations increasingly

adopt diverse cloud platforms to optimize infrastructure and avoid dependence on a single vendor, the support system should be versatile enough to manage these varied environments effectively.

4. **Automation and Monitoring:** Implementing automation and monitoring tools is crucial. This involves using cloud orchestration tools, automated provisioning systems, and monitoring and alerting systems. These technologies help streamline tasks and rapidly identify and address issues, enhancing the efficiency of support processes.
5. **Collaborative Support:** Encouraging collaboration among various IT teams, including development, operations, and security, is key. This collaborative approach ensures that support processes are integrated and consistently aligned with the organization's business goals.
6. **Compliance and Security:** Maintaining compliance and ensuring security in the cloud environment are imperative. The support model must incorporate robust security measures, such as stringent access controls and data encryption. Additionally, it's crucial to ensure that cloud infrastructure and operations comply with relevant industry regulations and standards. This dual focus on compliance and security protects the organization's data and infrastructure and aligns with regulatory expectations.

A well-structured support model post-cloud migration is crucial to manage and maximize the potential of the organization's cloud infrastructure effectively. Here are the reasons why such a support model is essential:

1. **Management:** Managing cloud infrastructure involves complex processes and requires ongoing attention to ensure optimal functionality. A structured support model equips an organization with the necessary tools, processes, and expertise

for effective management. This includes tasks like routine monitoring, maintenance, and quick troubleshooting.

2. **Security:** With the growing prevalence of cyber threats, ensuring robust security for cloud infrastructure is imperative. A comprehensive support model is needed to implement strong security measures like access controls, data encryption, and network segmentation, safeguarding applications and sensitive data against potential cyber threats.
3. **Optimization:** Cloud infrastructure offers opportunities for optimization in both performance and cost-efficiency. A support model helps in identifying and addressing underutilized resources or inefficiencies, employing tools and strategies like cost management systems, capacity planning, and load balancing to optimize operations.
4. **Compliance:** Compliance with various regulations and standards, such as HIPAA, GDPR, or PCI DSS, is vital for cloud infrastructure. A support model aids in ensuring adherence to these regulations by implementing necessary security measures and maintaining essential documentation and records.
5. **Business Continuity:** A solid support model is critical for maintaining business continuity in the event of disasters or system failures. It includes developing robust disaster recovery plans and implementing effective backup and recovery mechanisms to minimize downtime and data loss.
6. **Collaboration:** Cloud infrastructure necessitates collaboration among various IT teams, including development, operations, and security. A well-defined support model promotes this inter-departmental collaboration, ensuring that the support processes are well-integrated and aligned with the overarching business objectives.

CHAPTER 27

New Cloud Infrastructure Teams

After migrating to the cloud, organizations often need to form specialized cloud infrastructure teams to effectively manage and optimize their new cloud-based resources. These teams play a crucial role in ensuring that the cloud infrastructure is secure, compliant, and aligned with the organization's business objectives. Here are the key roles typically required in these new cloud infrastructure teams:

1. **Cloud Infrastructure Manager:** This role involves overseeing the entire cloud infrastructure of the organization. The Cloud Infrastructure Manager is responsible for making sure that the cloud environment is secure, scalable, and optimized for both performance and cost. They manage the overall cloud strategy, including the design and implementation of cloud solutions.
2. **Cloud Architect:** The Cloud Architect's job is to design the cloud infrastructure, ensuring it meets the organization's needs. They select appropriate cloud services, handle integration requirements, and ensure customizations align with business

goals. Their expertise is critical in designing a cloud environment that supports the organization's strategic objectives.

3. **Cloud Operations Engineer:** This role involves the day-to-day management of the cloud environment. The Cloud Operations Engineer monitors the infrastructure, troubleshoots issues, and optimizes for performance and cost. They play a key role in maintaining the smooth operation of cloud services.
4. **Cloud Security Engineer:** A vital role, the Cloud Security Engineer focuses on the security aspects of the cloud infrastructure. They implement robust security measures like access control, encryption, and network segmentation, and ensure compliance with relevant standards and regulations to protect against cyber threats.
5. **Cloud Automation Engineer:** This role focuses on enhancing efficiency through automation. The Cloud Automation Engineer develops scripts and tools to automate routine cloud management tasks. Their work streamlines processes such as provisioning, deployment, and maintenance, contributing to overall operational efficiency.
6. **Cloud Cost Analyst:** The Cloud Cost Analyst monitors and analyzes cloud spending. Their role is to identify underutilized resources, oversee resource usage, and implement strategies to optimize costs. They are key in ensuring that the cloud infrastructure is not only effective but also cost-efficient.

The creation of specialized cloud infrastructure teams post-cloud migration is essential to ensure the effective management, optimization, and security of an organization's cloud-based resources. These teams bring a focused approach and specific skills to handle various aspects of the cloud environment. Here are the key reasons for forming these new cloud infrastructure teams:

1. **Specialized Skills:** Cloud environments demand a distinct set of skills and knowledge, often not present in traditional IT teams. New cloud infrastructure teams bring specialized

expertise in managing and optimizing cloud resources, which is crucial for effective cloud management.

2. **Focus:** These teams are solely focused on the cloud infrastructure, enabling them to concentrate exclusively on managing and enhancing cloud resources. This focus ensures that the cloud infrastructure aligns with business objectives and is maintained at an optimal level for performance and cost-efficiency.
3. **Scalability:** One of the major advantages of cloud infrastructure is its scalability. New cloud teams are adept at managing this scalability, ensuring the organization can swiftly adjust its resource usage in line with fluctuating business demands, thus optimizing overall resource utilization.
4. **Security:** The heightened need for security in the cloud is addressed by these teams. They implement critical security measures, including access controls, encryption, and network security, to safeguard applications and data against cyber threats, a vital aspect in the digital era.
5. **Cost Optimization:** Cloud infrastructure offers opportunities for cost optimization by eliminating inefficiencies and underutilized resources. These teams play a key role in identifying and implementing strategies to reduce cloud expenses, thereby contributing to the financial efficiency of cloud operations.
6. **Integration:** Ensuring that cloud infrastructure works harmoniously with existing IT systems is crucial. New cloud teams manage this integration effectively, aligning the cloud infrastructure with existing applications, data, and services to create a cohesive and efficient IT environment.

CHAPTER 28

Server Costing Analysis

After migrating to a cloud environment, conducting a server costing analysis is crucial for an organization to gain a clear understanding of the expenses associated with operating their servers. This analysis plays a pivotal role in various aspects of cloud management and optimization. Here are the key reasons why server costing analysis is important post-migration:

1. **Cost Optimization:** By closely examining the expenses related to running servers in the cloud, organizations can pinpoint areas where they may be spending excessively. This analysis facilitates the identification of underutilized resources or inefficiencies, allowing for adjustments that can lead to significant cost reductions while maintaining optimal server performance.
2. **Budgeting:** Understanding the actual costs of cloud server operations is fundamental for accurate financial planning. With detailed insights from server costing analysis, organizations can forecast budgets more precisely, ensuring they allocate appropriate resources for their cloud operations. This accuracy is vital for maintaining financial health and planning future investments or expansions.

3. **Vendor Comparison:** Server costing analysis offers valuable data for comparing the costs of operating servers across different cloud platforms. Organizations can use this information to assess which cloud vendor offers the best value, considering factors like performance, cost, and additional services. This comparison is essential for making informed decisions about potential migrations or diversifications of cloud services.
4. **SLA Compliance:** Regular server costing analysis ensures that the organization's cloud infrastructure aligns with the agreed terms in their Service Level Agreements (SLAs) with cloud providers. By monitoring costs, organizations can verify if they are receiving the service levels they are paying for and address any discrepancies with their providers.
5. **Optimization of Cloud Resources:** This analysis is not just about cost-cutting; it's also about maximizing the efficiency of cloud resources. By understanding the cost implications of their current server usage, organizations can make informed decisions about scaling up or down their resources. This approach ensures that they are not over-provisioning (which leads to unnecessary costs) or under-provisioning (which could hamper performance).

When assessing the financial implications of operating servers in a cloud environment, a systematic server costing analysis is vital. This process involves a series of steps that enable organizations to understand and manage their cloud expenses effectively. Here's a structured approach to conducting such an analysis:

1. **Identify Server Configuration:** Begin by evaluating the specific configurations of the servers under consideration for cloud deployment. Key aspects to identify include the required processing power (CPU), memory (RAM), storage capacity, and network setup. This step forms the basis for understanding the resource needs and corresponding costs.

2. **Determine Cloud Provider Pricing:** Once you have a clear picture of the server requirements, the next step is to explore the pricing models offered by various cloud service providers. This investigation should encompass the costs associated with diverse cloud services relevant to your server configuration, such as the pricing for compute power, storage solutions, and network services. It's crucial to note that cloud providers often have different pricing tiers and discounts for long-term commitments, which should be taken into account.
3. **Estimate Usage:** Estimate how much the server will be utilized over a set period, like a month or a year. This estimation should consider factors such as the expected operational hours of the server, the volume of data storage, and the extent of data transfer (both inbound and outbound). Accurate usage projections are key to understanding the cost implications over time.
4. **Calculate Total Cost:** With the pricing details and usage estimates at hand, calculate the total cost of operating the server in the cloud. This calculation should aggregate the costs of compute resources, storage, and networking, based on the estimated usage patterns. This step provides a comprehensive view of the financial commitment involved in cloud server operation.
5. **Cost Comparison:** The final step is a comparative analysis between the costs of cloud-based and in-house server operations. This comparison should factor in not only the direct costs of running the server in the cloud but also the costs associated with in-house server maintenance, including hardware purchase, power consumption, cooling requirements, and ongoing maintenance.

CHAPTER 29

Instances Costing Analysis

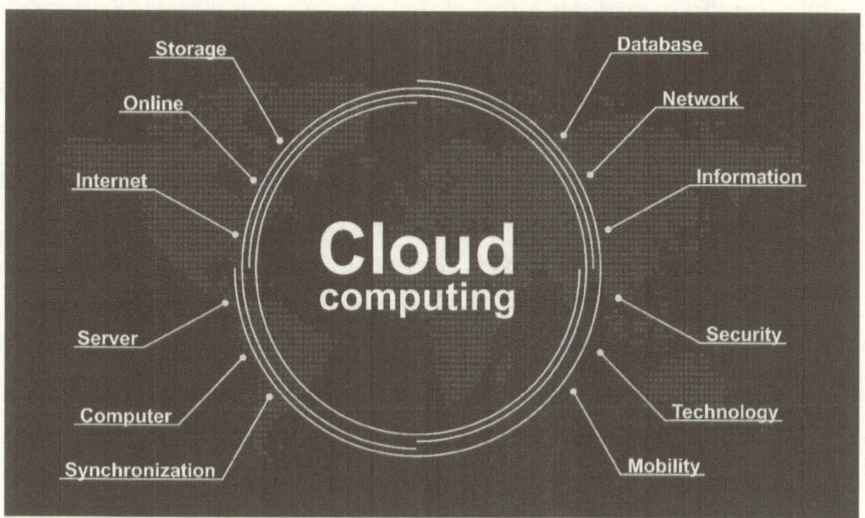

Carrying out an instance costing analysis is crucial for comprehending the expenses involved in operating virtual machines within a cloud framework. This analysis provides a clear picture of financial commitments and aids in making informed decisions about cloud services. The process for conducting this analysis can be outlined in the following steps:

1. **Identify Instance Configuration:** Begin by thoroughly assessing the specific configuration requirements for the instance in question. Key elements to consider are the processing power (CPU), memory (RAM), storage needs, and the network setup. This step is fundamental in understanding the resource requirements which directly impact the cost.
2. **Determine Cloud Provider Pricing:** Once the instance configuration is clearly defined, the next step involves exploring

the pricing structures offered by cloud service providers for those specific configurations. This exploration should cover different types of instances, such as those optimized for general purposes, those that are memory-intensive, and those designed for high computational tasks. Cloud service providers often offer varied pricing for different instance types, which needs careful consideration.

3. **Estimate Usage:** After pinpointing the type of instance and the provider's pricing, estimate the extent of usage for a set timeframe, such as monthly or yearly. This should include predictions about the number of operational hours of the instance and the scale of data storage and transfer involved.
4. **Calculate Total Cost:** With the configuration, pricing, and usage estimations in hand, proceed to calculate the total cost of operating the instance in the cloud. This calculation should encompass the costs associated with the instance itself, along with storage and networking, all multiplied by the estimated usage. This step yields an overall cost projection for running the instance in a cloud setup.
5. **Compare Costs:** The final stage involves a comparative analysis of the cost of operating the instance in the cloud versus an in-house setup. This should compare the total cloud operation costs with the expenses of purchasing, operating, and maintaining a similar instance in-house. This comparison is critical in evaluating the financial viability and benefits of cloud migration for the specific instance.

PHASE 6

MANAGING CLOUD PHASE

CHAPTER 30

Cloud Managed Services

The Cloud Managed Services phase in cloud migration is a crucial stage where an organization collaborates with a cloud service provider to oversee and maintain their cloud-based infrastructure and services. During this phase, the responsibility of managing and operating the cloud environment, encompassing infrastructure, applications, and data, is undertaken by the cloud service provider.

In Cloud Managed Services, the range and extent of services offered can vary, tailored to the specific requirements of the organization and the expertise of the service provider. The services commonly included are:

1. **Cloud Infrastructure Management:** The service provider assumes control over the organization's cloud infrastructure, which includes handling resources such as computing power, storage capacity, and network functionalities. Key tasks include the setup, configuration, and fine-tuning of these resources to strike a balance between performance efficiency and cost-effectiveness.
2. **Application Management:** This involves the service provider taking charge of cloud-based applications, encompassing their installation, configuration, and regular maintenance. The focus here is on maintaining security, ensuring high performance, and aligning these applications with the strategic objectives of the organization.
3. **Data Management:** The service provider manages critical data processes such as data backup, replication, and archival. The aim is to keep the data secure, in compliance with regulations, and readily available for access and use.
4. **Security and Compliance:** The service provider is tasked with ensuring robust security and compliance measures for the cloud infrastructure. This includes the implementation of stringent security protocols, like access control measures, data encryption, and network segmentation, while also ensuring adherence to relevant regulatory standards and laws.
5. **Monitoring and Support:** The service provider engages in continuous monitoring and support activities for the cloud environment. This encompasses prompt identification and resolution of any arising issues, optimization for both performance and cost-efficiency, and ensuring the continuity of business operations, particularly in disaster scenarios.

CHAPTER 31

Ticketing and Support

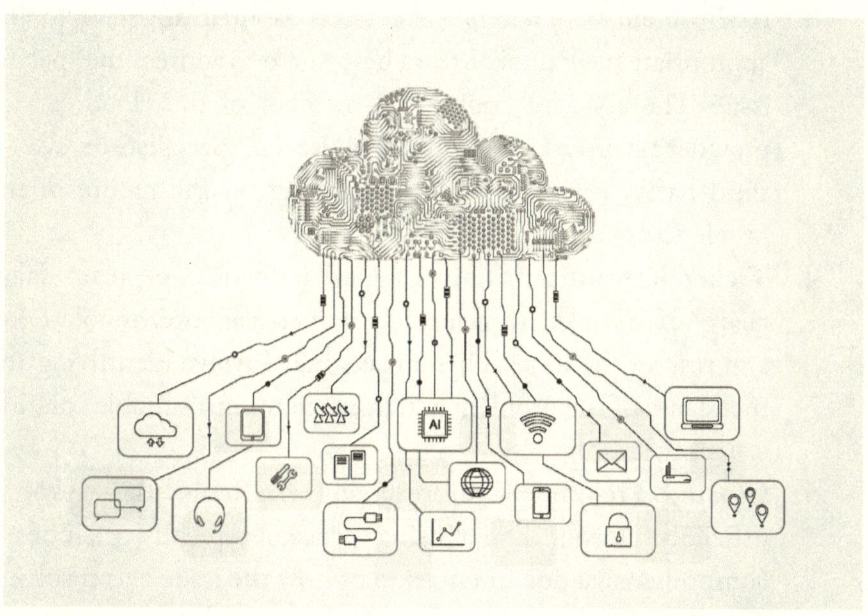

During the Cloud Managed Services phase, a structured ticketing and support system is crucial for efficiently managing and resolving issues within an organization's cloud environment. This process typically involves several key steps:

1. **Creation of Tickets:** Whenever an issue arises in the cloud environment, it triggers the creation of a support ticket. This can be initiated either by the organization's IT team or the cloud service provider's support team. The ticket contains crucial details about the issue, including its severity, specific location within the cloud infrastructure, and the potential impact it has on business operations.

2. **Prioritizing Tickets:** Once a ticket is logged, it is then prioritized based on the urgency and the potential impact on the organization's operations. High-priority tickets, typically those involving critical issues affecting key operations, are escalated for immediate action. Less critical issues are queued with lower priority.
3. **Assignment of Tickets:** The ticket is then assigned to the appropriate personnel or team best suited to address the specific issue. The assignee could be a member of the cloud service provider's support team, an in-house IT specialist, or even a third-party service provider, depending on the nature of the problem.
4. **Ticket Resolution:** The assigned individual or team takes charge of the ticket, working diligently to diagnose, troubleshoot, and resolve the issue. This process may involve identifying the root cause of the problem and implementing a suitable solution to rectify it.
5. **Closing Tickets:** After resolving the issue, the ticket is officially closed. The closing process typically includes a comprehensive documentation of how the issue was resolved, detailing the root cause analysis, the actions taken to fix the problem, and any recommendations for preventing similar issues in the future.
6. **Ticket Reporting:** Finally, the ticketing system is used as a tool for tracking and analyzing the performance and efficiency of the support process. Key metrics such as the volume of tickets, the average time taken to resolve issues, and the level of customer satisfaction are monitored to assess the effectiveness of the support system.

The ticketing and support process in the Cloud Managed Services phase plays a pivotal role in ensuring swift and effective resolution of issues, thereby minimizing their impact on business operations. It enables organizations to maintain a high level of service quality and operational continuity in their cloud environment.

Establishing an efficient ticketing and support process during the Cloud Managed Services phase is essential for maintaining a robust cloud environment. This process involves several key steps to ensure that support is timely, effective, and aligns with organizational needs:

1. **Defining Service Level Agreements (SLAs):** The foundation of a good support process begins with clear SLAs. These agreements should detail the expected levels of support, including the severity classifications for different issues, corresponding response times, and detailed escalation paths for urgent or critical problems.
2. **Identifying Support Teams:** It's crucial to clearly outline the composition and structure of the support teams. This involves defining the roles and responsibilities of each team member and establishing effective communication channels for efficient issue escalation and resolution.
3. **Selecting a Ticketing System:** Choosing the right ticketing system is a pivotal step. The selected system should be user-friendly, reliable, and feature-rich to handle the complexities of the support process. It should enable easy ticket logging, tracking, and management.
4. **Developing Ticketing and Support Procedures:** Develop comprehensive procedures that outline the entire ticketing and support process. These procedures should include guidelines for ticket creation, prioritization, assignment, resolution, and closure. Clear procedures ensure consistency and efficiency in handling support requests.
5. **Training Support Teams:** Providing thorough training to the support teams is critical. The training should cover the ticketing system, SLAs, support procedures, and the specific communication protocols to be followed. Well-trained teams can respond to and resolve issues more effectively.

6. **Monitoring and Improvement:** The final step involves regular monitoring of the support process and identifying areas for improvement. Key performance indicators like ticket resolution times, volume of tickets, and customer satisfaction should be continuously evaluated to refine and enhance the support process.

CHAPTER 32

Infrastructure Issues

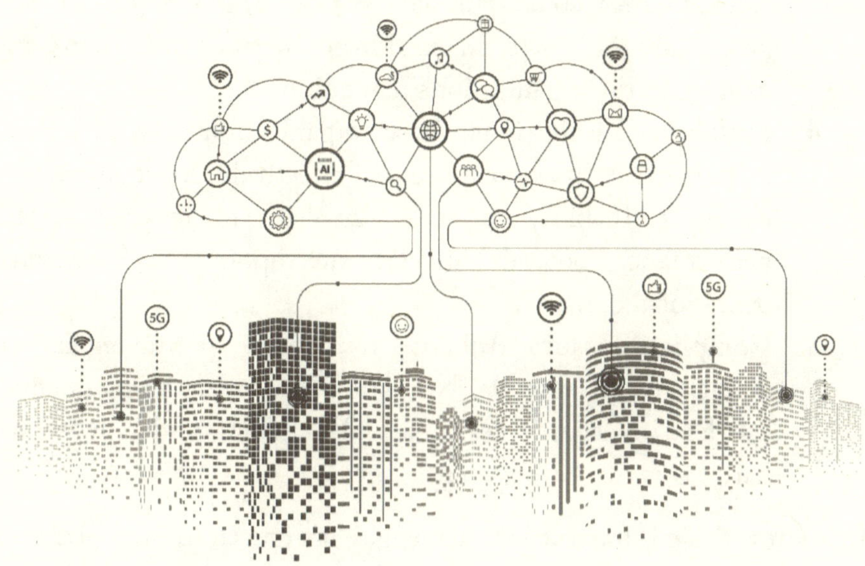

During the Cloud Managed Services phase, organizations might encounter various infrastructure challenges. Understanding and preparing for these common issues is crucial for maintaining a stable and efficient cloud environment:

1. **Performance Issues:** Performance problems can arise due to several factors, such as inadequate resource allocation, high network latency, or poorly optimized applications. These issues can affect the functionality and speed of cloud services, leading to a subpar experience for users and a potential decrease in operational productivity.
2. **Availability issues:** Issues related to service availability can disrupt access to cloud services. This can be caused by hardware malfunctions, software glitches, or other unforeseen

complications. Such disruptions can lead to significant operational downtime, potentially affecting the organization's revenue and workflow continuity.

3. **Security issues:** Security-related challenges might emerge due to reasons like improperly set security configurations, unauthorized access attempts, or malware attacks. These vulnerabilities could put data privacy and integrity at risk, potentially leading to financial losses, legal complications, and damage to the organization's reputation.
4. **Scalability Limitations:** As an organization grows, its cloud infrastructure may struggle to effectively meet increasing demands. Inability to scale can lead to reduced system performance, potential service interruptions, and escalated operational costs.
5. **Compliance issues:** Adhering to industry-specific regulations and standards is essential. Non-compliance with these guidelines can lead to legal issues, financial penalties, and reputational harm.

To address these infrastructure challenges, it's crucial for organizations to have robust monitoring and management systems in place. Regular performance and security monitoring, alongside proactive issue resolution strategies, are essential. Collaborating closely with cloud service providers to ensure that the cloud setup aligns with industry norms and best practices is also vital. Through diligent management and proactive issue mitigation, organizations can maintain an optimized, secure, and cost-effective cloud environment.

What causes these problems?

Infrastructure challenges in the Cloud Managed Services phase can arise from various sources. Understanding these underlying reasons is key to preventing and resolving such issues effectively:

1. **Insufficient Resources:** Performance problems in cloud infrastructure often stem from insufficient resource allocation,

like not having enough CPU, memory, or storage. This underprovisioning typically occurs when an organization fails to allocate resources adequately to match its operational demands.

2. **Configuration Errors:** Errors in configuring the infrastructure can lead to significant issues. This includes incorrectly set security parameters, network setups, or application configurations, which can adversely affect the cloud environment's availability, performance, and security.
3. **Ineffective Monitoring:** A lack of comprehensive monitoring and management can also lead to infrastructure issues. Without efficient monitoring systems in place, organizations might not detect problems until they significantly disrupt business operations.
4. **Lack of Expertise:** Challenges may arise due to a deficiency in cloud management expertise. If an organization lacks personnel with the necessary skills and knowledge to effectively oversee its cloud infrastructure, this can result in a range of issues, including those related to performance, availability, and security.
5. **Business Growth:** Issues related to scalability and availability often occur when an organization grows faster than its cloud infrastructure's capacity. This expansion can put excessive demands on the infrastructure, leading to a host of issues including reduced performance and potential service interruptions.

CHAPTER 33

Cloud Alert Notifications and Processes

Cloud alert notifications and processes are essential for maintaining the health and security of cloud-based resources. They function by continuously monitoring cloud resources and alerting relevant personnel if any predefined conditions or thresholds are breached. These alerts often focus on various performance indicators, such as CPU usage, memory consumption, network traffic, or response times of applications.

Setting up an efficient cloud alert notification system typically involves several key steps:

1. **Define Key Metrics and Thresholds:** Initially, it's crucial to identify which performance metrics are vital to monitor. Once these metrics are identified, appropriate thresholds are set. When these thresholds are crossed, an alert is triggered. Key metrics often include aspects like CPU usage, memory utilization, network bandwidth usage, and response times of critical applications.

2. **Choose a Monitoring Solution:** The next step involves choosing a monitoring tool compatible with the cloud environment. This tool should be capable of monitoring the chosen metrics and generating alerts when needed. Popular choices for these tools include Amazon CloudWatch for AWS, Azure Monitor for Microsoft Azure, and Google Cloud Monitoring for Google Cloud Platform.
3. **Configure Alerts:** After choosing a monitoring tool, the next phase involves configuring it to send alerts under specified conditions. These alerts can be set up to notify stakeholders through various channels, such as emails, text messages, or dedicated alerting systems.
4. **Define Escalation Procedures:** It is important to define clear escalation procedures for each type of alert. These protocols detail the actions to be taken when an alert is triggered, such as escalating the issue to specialized support teams, contacting external vendors, or initiating specific disaster recovery actions.
5. **Test and Refine:** Finally, it's critical to regularly test and adjust the alerting process to ensure its effectiveness. This process might involve conducting scenario-based tests to check alert responses and fine-tuning the monitoring thresholds, alert settings, or escalation procedures as required.

Creating an effective cloud alert notification system involves a systematic approach to ensure that critical issues are promptly identified and addressed. Here's a step-by-step guide to establish this system:

1. **Identification of Key Metrics and Thresholds:** Start by pinpointing crucial metrics that need monitoring and establish thresholds that, when crossed, will trigger alerts. These metrics are typically key performance indicators (KPIs) and service level objectives (SLOs) vital to the smooth operation of the organization. It could include metrics like response times, system uptime, error rates, or resource utilization levels.

2. **Choose a Monitoring Solution:** Choose a cloud monitoring tool that aligns with your organization's needs. This tool should be capable of tracking the identified metrics and generating alerts when their thresholds are breached. Important factors to consider include the tool's features, its integration capabilities with other systems, and its overall reliability. Tools like AWS CloudWatch, Azure Monitor, or Google Cloud Monitoring are popular choices, each offering unique features and integrations.
3. **Configure Alerts:** Set up the alert parameters within the chosen monitoring tool. This involves specifying what conditions will trigger an alert, determining how notifications will be sent (such as through email, SMS, or in-app notifications), and customizing the content of alert messages to ensure they convey the necessary information effectively.
4. **Establishment of Escalation Protocols:** Develop clear escalation procedures for handling alerts. This step is crucial for outlining how to respond when an alert is triggered. It should define the roles and responsibilities of team members, the steps for escalating issues to higher levels of support if needed, and criteria for determining the severity of an issue.
5. **Test and Refine:** Finally, rigorously test the alerting system to ensure its effectiveness. Simulate various scenarios to see how the system responds, examine the alert logs to understand the system's behavior, and adjust the monitoring thresholds, alert settings, or escalation processes based on these findings.

CHAPTER 34

Hybrid Teams Support Model

Implementing a Hybrid Teams Support Model offers a balanced approach to managing an organization's cloud environment, blending the expertise of internal IT teams with the specialized services of external vendors. This model is structured as follows:

1. **In-House IT Staff:** The core of the Hybrid Teams Support Model revolves around the organization's internal IT staff. These team members are primarily responsible for the routine management and operation of the cloud environment. Their tasks encompass monitoring the cloud infrastructure, maintaining applications and data, providing user support, and upholding stringent security and compliance measures.

2. **Third-Party Vendors:** External third-party vendors, including cloud service providers and specialized technology firms, play a crucial role in this model. They bring specific expertise and services that might be beyond the scope of the in-house team. These services often include managed cloud solutions, advanced security services, and custom application development. By engaging these vendors, organizations can tap into a broader range of cloud capabilities and innovations.
3. **Collaboration:** Successful execution of the Hybrid Teams Support Model hinges on effective collaboration between the in-house IT staff and third-party vendors. This partnership involves sharing responsibilities, exchanging knowledge, and jointly addressing the challenges of cloud management. Such collaborative efforts are instrumental in ensuring that the cloud infrastructure operates efficiently and any issues are promptly resolved.
4. **Flexibility:** A defining characteristic of this model is its adaptability. It allows organizations to dynamically scale their cloud support structure based on evolving business needs. This flexibility can manifest in varying the involvement of third-party vendors, adjusting support levels, or redistributing tasks between in-house staff and external experts as necessary.

The Hybrid Teams Support Model is particularly beneficial for organizations seeking the agility and innovation offered by cloud technologies while retaining substantial control over their cloud operations. This model not only leverages specialized external expertise but also provides the versatility to adapt to changing business landscapes, making it a strategic choice for modern, cloud-centric organizations.

The Hybrid Teams Support Model is crucial for organizations navigating the complexities of cloud technology. It offers a strategic approach by combining internal expertise with external proficiency. The necessity of this model is underscored by several key advantages:

1. **Expertise:** One of the primary advantages of this model is the specialized knowledge and skills offered by third-party vendors. These experts bring a wealth of experience in specific areas such as cloud security, regulatory compliance, and performance optimization. Their insights can significantly enhance an organization's ability to effectively manage and refine its cloud infrastructure.
2. **Scalability:** Managing an extensive cloud environment can be challenging, particularly for organizations with limited in-house capabilities. Third-party vendors offer the scalability needed to expand or contract cloud resources and support, depending on the organization's evolving requirements. This scalability is vital for accommodating fluctuating demands without overextending internal resources.
3. **Cost-Effective:** Building an in-house team capable of managing all aspects of a cloud environment can be costly, requiring significant investment in recruitment and training. The Hybrid Teams Support Model allows organizations to tap into the expertise of third-party vendors, often at a more manageable cost. This approach can be more economical than developing comprehensive in-house capabilities.
4. **Flexibility:** This model affords organizations the flexibility to adapt their cloud strategy as needs change. They can seamlessly integrate or disengage third-party services, modify support levels, and redistribute tasks between internal teams and external providers. This flexibility ensures that the cloud infrastructure remains aligned with the organization's dynamic business objectives.
5. **Rapid Response:** Third-party vendors typically have dedicated teams and resources focused on cloud management,

enabling them to swiftly identify and resolve issues. This rapid response capability is essential for minimizing downtime and mitigating the impact of any disruptions on business operations. Access to these dedicated resources ensures prompt and efficient issue resolution, a critical requirement in today's fast-paced business environment.

CHAPTER 35

Optimization Stage for Further Improvements

The Optimization stage in cloud migration is crucial as it represents the phase where organizations refine and enhance their cloud setup for superior performance, efficiency, and cost-effectiveness. It's a time for fine-tuning and perfecting the cloud environment using a variety of tools and strategies. This stage encompasses several key activities:

1. **Performance Optimization:** This activity focuses on using tools and techniques to enhance the performance of the cloud environment. It often involves adjusting the infrastructure for better results, optimizing application performance for faster

and smoother operation, and ensuring the network operates at its best.

2. **Cost Optimization:** Here, the goal is to identify and cut down on unnecessary expenses linked to the cloud setup. Activities often include pinpointing resources that are not being fully utilized, better allocating resources to match actual needs, and reducing wastage to save costs.
3. **Security Optimization:** This aspect is centered around strengthening the security of the cloud environment. It typically involves the implementation of stronger security measures, addressing any security weaknesses, and continuously monitoring the environment for new threats.
4. **Compliance Optimization:** Compliance optimization ensures that the cloud setup adheres to relevant industry regulations and standards. It often involves conducting thorough compliance checks, putting the necessary controls in place, and verifying that data management adheres to the required regulatory standards.
5. **Process Optimization:** This involves streamlining the processes and workflows that are part of managing the cloud environment. Key activities here include automating repetitive tasks, enhancing team communication and collaboration, and integrating best practices for more efficient cloud management.

The significance of the Optimization stage lies in its capacity to push the cloud environment beyond just functionality, into a realm where it delivers peak performance and maximum value. By carefully optimizing their cloud infrastructure, organizations not only make the most of their cloud investment but also align their cloud strategies more closely with their broader business goals and objectives. This stage is essential for ensuring that the transition to the cloud translates into tangible benefits for the organization.

Optimization plays a pivotal role in the success of cloud migration, ensuring that organizations maximize the potential of their cloud-based environment. The importance of optimization can be distilled into several key aspects:

1. **Enhanced Performance:** Through optimization, organizations can significantly boost the performance of their cloud setup. This involves fine-tuning the infrastructure for optimal operation, enhancing the performance of applications, and ensuring smooth and efficient network functioning. The outcome is a more reliable and swift cloud service, leading to enhanced productivity and organizational efficiency.
2. **Cost Efficiency:** A major advantage of optimization is the reduction of unnecessary cloud-related expenses. By pinpointing resources that are not fully utilized, reallocating resources more appropriately, and cutting down on wastage, organizations can reduce their expenditure on cloud services. This leads to a more cost-effective use of cloud technology and a better return on the initial investment.
3. **Better Security:** Optimization plays a crucial role in bolstering the security of a cloud environment. It involves identifying and rectifying security weaknesses, implementing robust security measures, and continuously monitoring for potential threats. This proactive approach to cloud security helps safeguard critical organizational data and maintains the integrity of the company's reputation.
4. **Compliance:** Adherence to industry regulations and standards is another critical aspect of cloud optimization. Through regular compliance checks, implementation of necessary compliance controls, and ensuring data is managed correctly, organizations can mitigate the risk of non-compliance penalties and legal issues. This is especially crucial for organizations dealing with sensitive data or operating in heavily regulated industries.
5. **Streamlined Processes:** Effective optimization also refines and enhances cloud management processes. By automating routine tasks, fostering better communication and teamwork,

and applying industry best practices in cloud management, organizations can realize a more streamlined and effective approach to managing their cloud resources. This not only improves the day-to-day operations but also positively impacts the broader business efficiency of the organization.

Conclusion

Phase 1 – Cloud Assessment:

This crucial initial phase involves evaluating the current IT setup to determine the viability and potential benefits of transitioning to cloud technology. Activities include a macro-level assessment, preparation of a detailed server list, comprehensive application assessment, readiness evaluation for migration, and exploration of different migration strategies. This phase is key to deciding the best cloud migration approach, such as a replace model, retiring outdated systems, or adopting a lift and shift method.

Phase 2 – Database Mapping with Applications:

In this phase, the focus is on aligning databases with corresponding applications and understanding the data dependencies between them. The goal is to foresee potential challenges and ensure smooth data transition to the cloud. Clustering plays a crucial role here, helping to effectively organize databases for easier management in the cloud setting.

Phase 3 – Mobilizing Phase:

Here, organizations develop a detailed plan for cloud migration and select a cloud provider through the RFP process. It involves choosing the right tools and services, conducting licensing and cost analysis, and assessing operational expenses and other financial considerations. Defining clear policies and establishing rules are also part of this phase, alongside conducting a landing zone assessment to verify the readiness of the cloud environment for the incoming workloads.

Phase 4 – Migration Phase:

This is the hands-on phase where the actual shift of workloads to the cloud takes place. It is divided into three sub-phases: Lift and Shift Migration, Simplex Data and Applications Migration, and Complex Applications and Databases Migration. The emphasis during this phase is on the effective migration of workloads, data security, and fine-tuning the cloud environment to meet specific organizational needs.

Phase 5 – Cloud Operate Phase:

In this critical stage, the focus shifts to the ongoing operation and management of the cloud environment. Organizations define a new operating model, incorporating elements like novel support frameworks, cloud infrastructure teams, and comprehensive server cost analyses. Additionally, instance costing analysis is performed to maximize cloud resource utilization and efficiency. This phase is pivotal in transitioning from migration to steady-state operations in the cloud, ensuring the infrastructure is not just functional but also optimized for organizational needs.

Phase 6 – Cloud Managed Services:

This phase is integral for maintaining and enhancing the cloud environment. Key activities include establishing robust ticketing and support processes, setting up cloud alert notifications, addressing infrastructure issues, and employing a hybrid teams support model. The ultimate goal in this stage is continual improvement and refinement, guaranteeing smooth, efficient, and cost-effective cloud operations. It's a phase where ongoing management melds with proactive enhancement, ensuring the cloud environment evolves in alignment with the organization's changing needs and goals.

In summary, cloud migration is a multifaceted and meticulous process. Each phase, from initial assessment to the continuous optimization in managed services, demands thorough planning and execution. It's not merely about shifting to the cloud but ensuring that every step enhances security, efficiency, and alignment with the organization's objectives. Properly navigated, this process unlocks the full spectrum of cloud computing benefits, mitigating risks and maximizing value from this transformational technology.

The journey through cloud migration is as intricate as it is rewarding. With each phase, from the groundwork of assessment to the fine-tuning of managed services, organizations traverse a path that reshapes not just their IT landscape but their operational ethos, paving the way for innovation, agility, and sustained growth in the cloud-centric era.

The effectiveness of transitioning to the cloud hinges on several critical elements, such as choosing an appropriate migration strategy, accurately evaluating the cloud ecosystem, and instituting new operational frameworks, support systems, and specialized cloud-focused teams.

Moreover, the journey to cloud proficiency is an evolving one, marked by continuous enhancements and meticulous cost management. This includes conducting thorough cost evaluations, analyzing the expenses associated with servers and virtual machines, setting up efficient cloud alert mechanisms, creating a hybrid support structure, and engaging in ongoing optimization processes. By adhering to a well-structured and carefully implemented cloud migration plan, organizations can significantly leverage the advantages of cloud computing, effectively navigating the complexities and potential pitfalls of this transformative journey.

CASE STUDIES

Case Studies in Australia

1. **Australian Securities Exchange (ASX):** In April 2021, ASX encountered technical difficulties while transitioning its equity market trading platform to a blockchain-based system. This complication resulted in a postponement of the new platform's launch.
2. **New South Wales Police Force:** During its cloud migration in May 2021, the New South Wales Police Force experienced operational challenges. These led to a brief halt of its online reporting system.
3. **Tabcorp:** Tabcorp, in May 2021, navigated obstacles in its cloud migration process, particularly in data migration and the integration with its existing legacy systems.
4. **Victorian Department of Education and Training:** The Victorian Department of Education and Training, in July 2021, encountered hurdles in its cloud migration process, leading to a temporary disruption of its online learning platform.
5. **Australian Broadcasting Corporation (ABC):** ABC faced technical disruptions in August 2021 during its transition of radio broadcasting systems to a new cloud-based platform, causing interruptions in its broadcasting services.
6. **Monash University:** In May 2020, Monash University faced significant challenges in its cloud migration process, which led to substantial delays in rolling out its new student management system.
7. **Australian Red Cross:** The Australian Red Cross, in July 2020, confronted difficulties in its cloud migration, particularly with data migration and blending these processes with its existing legacy systems.
8. **Service NSW:** In August 2020, Service NSW experienced disruptions during its cloud migration process, resulting in a

temporary suspension of various online services, including its COVID-19 hotline and appointment scheduling system.

9. **Australian National University:** In September 2020, the Australian National University encountered difficulties in its transition to cloud computing, experiencing complications in data migration and the merging of these processes with its pre-existing legacy systems.
10. **Australia Post:** Australia Post, in November 2020, navigated through obstacles in its cloud migration process, which resulted in considerable delays in rolling out its new parcel sorting technology.
11. **Bank of Queensland:** The Bank of Queensland, in November 2020, grappled with challenges during its shift to cloud computing, particularly in transferring data and incorporating these changes with its existing legacy systems.
12. **Westpac:** Westpac confronted issues in its cloud migration process in December 2020, mainly concerning data migration and the integration of these efforts with its pre-existing systems.
13. **National Australia Bank (NAB):** Throughout 2019, NAB encountered hurdles in its journey towards cloud computing, facing problems related to data migration and the harmonization of these processes with its legacy systems.
14. **Telstra:** In 2019, Telstra experienced difficulties during its shift to cloud technology, predominantly in the areas of data migration and integrating these changes with its existing legacy systems.
15. **Australia and New Zealand Banking Group (ANZ):** ANZ, in 2019, dealt with obstacles in its cloud migration journey, mainly concerning the migration of data and fitting these processes into its current legacy systems.
16. **Department of Defence:** The Department of Defence, in 2018, faced challenges while transitioning to cloud computing, leading to issues in data migration and combining these efforts with its existing systems.

17. **Optus:** In 2020, Optus suffered a significant service disruption due to a technical problem in its cloud infrastructure. This issue led to a widespread outage affecting many of its services, including the Optus website and mobile application.
18. **Woolworths:** In 2020, Woolworths encountered hurdles in its journey to cloud migration, which primarily involved complications in transferring data and integrating these new processes with its pre-existing legacy systems.
19. **University of Western Australia:** The University of Western Australia faced significant challenges in its cloud migration endeavors in 2018. Key issues included the complexities of migrating data and ensuring seamless integration with its existing legacy systems.
20. **Suncorp:** During 2019, Suncorp navigated through challenges in its shift to cloud computing, particularly in the areas of data migration and fitting these new processes into its established legacy systems.
21. **Australia and New Zealand Banking Group (ANZ):** ANZ in 2020 experienced difficulties in its cloud migration journey. The bank's challenges revolved around transferring data and merging these processes with its existing systems.
22. **NBN Co.:** In 2019, NBN Co. was confronted with obstacles in its move to the cloud, which resulted in significant delays in rolling out its new network services.
23. **Coles:** Coles, in 2019, grappled with challenges during its transition to cloud computing. The issues were centered on data migration and the integration of these efforts with its legacy systems.
24. **National Broadband Network (NBN):** NBN encountered notable challenges in its cloud migration process in 2020, leading to substantial delays in the implementation of its new network services.

25. **BHP:** In 2019, BHP faced hurdles in its cloud migration journey, dealing with issues related to data migration and the harmonization of these new processes with its existing legacy systems.

Case Studies in Canada

1. **Hydro One:** In January 2020, Hydro One encountered significant technical difficulties while transitioning its customer billing system to a new cloud-based platform. This shift resulted in delayed billing processes, leading to an influx of customer complaints.
2. **Air Canada:** August 2020 saw Air Canada grappling with challenges in its cloud migration efforts. This transition phase caused service disruptions that adversely affected thousands of its passengers.
3. **City of Toronto:** In August 2020, the City of Toronto experienced complications in its journey to cloud migration. The issues encountered led to the temporary suspension of various online services provided by the city.
4. **Canada Revenue Agency (CRA):** During its cloud migration process in August 2020, the CRA was hit by a cyber attack. This attack exacerbated the strain on its online services, already burdened by the ongoing migration.
5. **National Research Council of Canada (NRC):** The NRC faced significant obstacles in September 2020 during its transition to cloud computing. These challenges forced the temporary shutdown of its online services.
6. **Telus:** In October 2020, Telus confronted several issues amidst its cloud migration journey. The complications led to service disruptions, impacting thousands of its customers.
7. **Bank of Montreal (BMO):** BMO's cloud migration process in November 2020 was marked by difficulties that resulted in service disruptions, affecting numerous customers.
8. **Royal Bank of Canada (RBC):** RBC, in January 2021, faced hurdles in its cloud migration journey. The challenges encountered led to service interruptions, affecting a large number of its customers.

9. **Canada Post:** Canada Post's cloud migration in February 2021 was not smooth sailing. The organization struggled with data migration and the integration of these processes with its legacy systems.
10. **National Bank of Canada:** In March 2021, the National Bank of Canada experienced issues during its transition to cloud computing, leading to service disruptions that affected thousands of customers.
11. **Vancouver Coastal Health:** April 2021 saw Vancouver Coastal Health grappling with challenges in its cloud migration, leading to the temporary suspension of its online services.
12. **Canadian Imperial Bank of Commerce (CIBC):** CIBC, in May 2021, encountered obstacles in its cloud migration journey, resulting in service disruptions impacting a significant customer base.
13. **Ontario Ministry of Health:** The Ontario Ministry of Health faced difficulties in its cloud migration journey in May 2021, leading to a temporary halt in its online services.
14. **Hydro-Québec:** June 2021 was a challenging period for Hydro-Québec in its cloud migration journey, marked by issues that necessitated a temporary suspension of its online services.
15. **Canadian Broadcasting Corporation (CBC):** CBC encountered technical complications in June 2021 during the transition of its radio broadcasting systems to a cloud-based platform. These issues led to interruptions in broadcasting services, impacting their operations.
16. **Ontario Teachers' Pension Plan (OTPP):** In July 2021, OTPP's cloud migration effort was met with significant challenges. The organization struggled with migrating data and integrating it effectively with their existing legacy systems, posing hurdles in their digital transformation journey.

17. **National Defence and the Canadian Armed Forces:** The cloud migration process for National Defence and the Canadian Armed Forces in August 2021 was fraught with difficulties. The primary challenges they faced involved data migration and ensuring seamless integration with their longstanding legacy systems.
18. **Toronto Dominion Bank (TD):** September 2021 was a challenging period for TD during its migration to cloud-based systems. The bank encountered issues that disrupted its services, adversely affecting thousands of its customers.
19. **Canadian Natural Resources Limited (CNRL):** CNRL's transition to cloud computing in October 2021 was not without its hurdles. The company faced significant challenges related to data migration and integrating these new cloud processes with their existing legacy systems.
20. **Ontario Provincial Police (OPP):** The cloud migration journey for the OPP in November 2021 encountered obstacles that led to the temporary suspension of their online services. These challenges highlighted the complexities involved in migrating critical law enforcement and public safety operations to a cloud environment.

Case Studies in India

1. **State Bank of India:** In 2019, the State Bank of India (SBI) faced a significant operational disruption. Customers were unable to access their accounts or use online banking services due to a system outage. This problem originated from complications encountered during the transition to a new cloud-based system.
2. **HDFC Bank:** HDFC Bank encountered a critical system failure in 2020. This outage hindered customers' ability to access their accounts and disrupted online banking services, stemming from a technical issue within the bank's cloud infrastructure.
3. **Air India:** Air India faced a severe security issue in 2021 when it suffered a data breach. This breach compromised the personal information of millions of customers, attributed to a vulnerability in their cloud-based data storage system.
4. **National Stock Exchange of India:** The National Stock Exchange of India (NSE) experienced a technical malfunction in 2021. This issue disrupted trading activities and impeded investors' access to the platform. It was linked to challenges in migrating to a new cloud-based trading system.
5. **Canara Bank:** Canara Bank's online banking services faced a major interruption in 2020. Customers found themselves unable to access their accounts due to a system outage caused by a technical glitch in the bank's cloud infrastructure.
6. **Tata Consultancy Services:** Tata Consultancy Services (TCS) experienced a significant security breach in 2020. The breach led to the exposure of personal information of some employees, which was due to a vulnerability in TCS's cloud-based email system.
7. **Zomato:** In 2021, Zomato, a widely-used food delivery service in India, faced a major data breach. This incident exposed the personal information of millions of its customers, resulting from a security vulnerability in the company's cloud infrastructure.

8. **Airtel:** Airtel, a leading telecom provider in India, encountered a substantial system outage in 2020. This disruption affected their services, preventing customers from making calls or accessing data. The cause was identified as a technical issue within Airtel's cloud infrastructure.
9. **Bank of Baroda:** In 2019, Bank of Baroda encountered a major system disruption that affected its online banking services. Customers were unable to access their accounts due to this outage, which was traced back to complications in transitioning to a new cloud-based platform.
10. **Indian Railways:** Indian Railways faced a significant operational setback in 2019. A major system outage disrupted train services, leaving passengers without access to journey information. This issue was linked to difficulties encountered during the shift to a new cloud-based system.
11. **Punjab National Bank:** Punjab National Bank (PNB) experienced a system malfunction in 2021, severely disrupting its online banking services. Customers found themselves unable to access their accounts, a problem caused by technical challenges within the bank's cloud infrastructure.
12. **Apollo Hospitals:** In 2021, Apollo Hospitals, a prominent healthcare provider in India, faced a system outage. This incident disrupted patient care services and led to appointment delays. The cause was identified as issues during the migration to a new electronic health records system.
13. **Axis Bank:** Axis Bank encountered a system failure in 2020, affecting its online banking services. This disruption, preventing customer account access, was due to technical problems in the bank's cloud infrastructure.
14. **Ola:** Ola, a widely-used ride-hailing service in India, faced a system outage in 2021. This issue disrupted its services, hindering customers from booking rides. The problem originated from a technical glitch in the company's cloud infrastructure.

15. **IDFC First Bank:** In 2021, IDFC First Bank suffered a system outage, impacting its online banking services. This issue, which blocked customer account access, was caused by a technical fault in the bank's cloud infrastructure.
16. **Indian Institute of Technology (IIT) Bombay:** IIT Bombay experienced a system failure in 2021, disrupting online classes and blocking student access to course materials. The cause was identified as a technical problem in the institute's cloud infrastructure.
17. **Flipkart:** Flipkart, a leading e-commerce platform in India, faced a system outage in 2019. This issue disrupted online shopping services, preventing customer access to the platform, and was attributed to a technical problem with the company's cloud infrastructure.
18. **LIC Housing Finance:** In 2019, LIC Housing Finance underwent a system outage that interrupted its online banking services, restricting customer access to accounts. The cause was technical difficulties in the company's cloud-based system.
19. **Yes Bank:** Yes Bank experienced a system disruption in 2020, affecting its online banking services. Customers were unable to access their accounts due to technical problems in the bank's cloud infrastructure.
20. **Indian Space Research Organization (ISRO):** In 2019, ISRO faced a critical technical glitch during a lunar mission, leading to a loss of communication with the spacecraft. The glitch was linked to software issues related to the transition of vital systems to cloud computing.

Case Studies in USA

1. **Capital One:** In 2019, Capital One encountered a severe data breach following its cloud migration, exposing sensitive information of over 100 million customers. The breach was attributed to a misconfigured firewall within their cloud infrastructure, enabling a hacker to access customer data.
2. **State of California:** The state of California faced significant obstacles during its cloud migration in 2020, leading to delays in implementing its new state payroll system. Challenges included difficulties with data migration and integrating with existing legacy systems, compounded by a lack of cloud technology expertise.
3. **Target:** Target experienced a substantial data breach in 2013 due to a vulnerability within its cloud infrastructure. The incident led to the theft of over 40 million credit and debit card numbers and other sensitive information.
4. **Delta Airlines:** Delta Airlines suffered a major outage in 2017 caused by a power failure in its data center. This led to widespread flight cancellations and delays. Investigations revealed that the airline's backup systems also failed, hindering swift recovery efforts.
5. **IRS:** The Internal Revenue Service (IRS) encountered several problems during its 2019 cloud migration, resulting in the temporary shutdown of some tax processing systems. Issues with data migration and unexpected technical glitches caused delays in processing tax refunds and other services.
6. **Amazon Web Services:** In 2017, Amazon Web Services (AWS) experienced a significant outage due to human error during routine maintenance. This incident impacted many major websites and services, including Netflix, Spotify, and Airbnb.

7. **Marriott International:** In 2018, Marriott International was hit by a data breach stemming from vulnerabilities in its Starwood reservation system. This breach compromised the personal information of over 500 million customers, including names, addresses, phone numbers, and passport details.
8. **Anthem Inc.:** Anthem Inc. suffered a data breach in 2015 due to vulnerabilities in its cloud infrastructure. This breach exposed sensitive information of over 78 million customers, including names, birth dates, social security numbers, and other personal details.
9. **Dropbox:** Dropbox faced a significant service outage in 2012 caused by a bug in its synchronization service. Millions of users were affected, unable to access their files and documents.
10. **Sony Pictures:** Sony Pictures experienced a massive data breach in 2014 due to vulnerabilities in its IT infrastructure. The breach led to the exposure of sensitive information of over 100 million customers, including names, addresses, phone numbers, and email addresses.
11. **JPMorgan Chase:** In 2014, JPMorgan Chase encountered a significant data breach due to a vulnerability in its network infrastructure. This incident led to the unauthorized access and theft of sensitive data from over 76 million households and 7 million small businesses.
12. **Twitter:** In 2016, Twitter experienced a major outage attributed to a technical issue within its data center. This disruption impacted millions of users, hindering access to their accounts and the ability to post tweets.
13. **The New York Times:** The New York Times in 2013 faced a substantial service interruption due to a technical problem in its data center. This issue temporarily halted the publication of its digital edition for several hours.

14. **Etsy:** Etsy encountered a significant service disruption in 2018, caused by a bug within its infrastructure. This outage affected various major websites and services, including Etsy's own online platform and mobile application.
15. **HealthCare.gov:** In 2013, HealthCare.gov struggled with severe technical difficulties amid its cloud migration efforts. These challenges obstructed many users from registering for health insurance under the Affordable Care Act.
16. **GitHub:** GitHub experienced a major service outage in 2018, triggered by a DDoS attack targeting its cloud infrastructure. This incident disrupted access for millions of users, preventing them from reaching their code repositories.
17. **Slack:** In 2019, Slack suffered a significant service disruption due to a technical issue within its cloud infrastructure. This outage impacted millions of users, blocking access to their communication channels and messages.
18. **Delta Dental:** Delta Dental faced several obstacles during its 2020 cloud migration journey, encountering issues in data migration and integration with existing legacy systems.
19. **Macy's:** In 2019, Macy's experienced a notable service outage caused by a technical problem in its cloud infrastructure. The incident affected several major websites, hindering customers from completing their purchases.
20. **Adobe Creative Cloud:** Adobe Creative Cloud faced a substantial service disruption in 2019 due to a technical glitch in its cloud infrastructure. This outage impacted millions of users, restricting access to their creative tools and applications.

Case Studies in Japan

1. **Mizuho Bank:** In March 2021, Mizuho Bank encountered severe technical problems during the transition of its core banking system to a new cloud-based platform. This issue caused significant service disruptions, adversely affecting thousands of customers.
2. **Sumitomo Mitsui Banking Corporation (SMBC):** SMBC, in May 2021, faced complications during its transition to cloud computing, resulting in service interruptions that impacted numerous customers.
3. **Rakuten Mobile:** In June 2021, Rakuten Mobile experienced difficulties in its cloud migration process, leading to service disruptions that affected a large customer base.
4. **Softbank:** Softbank confronted challenges in its cloud migration journey in June 2021, leading to widespread service disruptions affecting thousands of its customers.
5. **Toyota Motor Corporation:** Toyota encountered obstacles during its cloud migration in July 2021, specifically in data migration and integration with existing legacy systems.
6. **Japan Post Bank:** Japan Post Bank in August 2021 faced technical challenges while transitioning its core banking system to a new cloud-based platform, resulting in significant service disruptions for many customers.
7. **Hitachi:** Hitachi experienced issues in its cloud migration process in August 2021, causing service disruptions that affected a large number of customers.
8. **Japan Airlines (JAL):** In September 2021, JAL faced hurdles in its cloud migration process, leading to service disruptions impacting thousands of customers.
9. **Mitsubishi UFJ Financial Group (MUFG):** MUFG encountered technical difficulties in October 2021 while migrating its core

banking system to a cloud-based platform, leading to service disruptions for numerous customers.

10. **NEC Corporation:** NEC Corporation experienced challenges in its cloud migration in October 2021, resulting in service disruptions that impacted many customers.
11. **NTT Communications:** In November 2021, NTT Communications faced issues during its cloud migration, leading to service interruptions that affected numerous customers.
12. **Mitsui & Co.:** Mitsui & Co. confronted challenges during its cloud migration in November 2021, particularly with data migration and integration with existing legacy systems.
13. **ANA Holdings:** ANA Holdings in December 2021 encountered technical problems during the migration of its booking system to a cloud-based platform, causing widespread service disruptions.
14. **Mitsubishi Electric Corporation:** In January 2022, Mitsubishi Electric faced difficulties in its cloud migration, leading to service interruptions impacting many customers.
15. **Nomura Holdings:** Nomura Holdings experienced technical issues in February 2022 while transitioning its core banking system to a cloud-based platform, causing service disruptions for numerous customers.
16. **JXTG Nippon Oil & Energy:** In March 2022, JXTG Nippon Oil & Energy faced challenges during its cloud migration, leading to service disruptions affecting a wide customer base.
17. **SBI Holdings:** SBI Holdings encountered technical difficulties in April 2022 during the migration of its core banking system to a cloud-based platform, resulting in service disruptions for many customers.
18. **Sony Corporation:** Sony faced hurdles in its cloud migration journey in May 2022, leading to service interruptions that impacted many customers.

19. **Fujitsu:** Fujitsu experienced technical challenges in June 2022 during the migration of its data center to a cloud-based platform, causing service disruptions affecting a large number of customers.
20. **Kobe Steel:** Kobe Steel confronted challenges in its cloud migration journey in July 2022, particularly with data migration and integration with existing legacy systems.

Case Studies in UK

1. **NatWest Bank:** In March 2021, NatWest Bank experienced significant technical difficulties during its transition to cloud computing. This disruption adversely affected its services, impacting numerous customers.
2. **Virgin Media:** Virgin Media encountered complications in its cloud migration in April 2021, leading to service interruptions that affected their customer base.
3. **Post Office:** The Post Office faced hurdles in its cloud migration project in May 2021, resulting in service disruptions and impacting customers.
4. **Lloyds Bank:** In June 2021, Lloyds Bank confronted technical issues during its cloud migration initiative, causing service disruptions that impacted a broad customer base.
5. **Marks & Spencer:** Marks & Spencer experienced challenges in its cloud migration process in July 2021, leading to service disruptions and customer impact.
6. **John Lewis:** In August 2021, John Lewis encountered difficulties during its cloud migration, resulting in service interruptions and customer inconveniences.
7. **Tesco Bank:** Tesco Bank faced technical challenges during its cloud migration in September 2021, causing service disruptions that affected numerous customers.
8. **TUI Group:** TUI Group confronted obstacles in its cloud migration process in October 2021, leading to service disruptions and customer impact.
9. **Santander Bank:** In November 2021, Santander Bank experienced technical difficulties during its cloud migration project, leading to service disruptions and customer inconveniences.
10. **British Gas:** British Gas faced cloud migration challenges in December 2021, resulting in service interruptions and customer impact.

11. **National Lottery:** The National Lottery encountered technical difficulties during its cloud migration in January 2022, leading to service disruptions and customer inconveniences.
12. **British Airways:** In February 2022, British Airways faced issues during its cloud migration, resulting in service disruptions and impacting customers.
13. **NHS Scotland:** NHS Scotland experienced challenges in its cloud migration in March 2022, causing service disruptions that affected patients.
14. **Scottish Power:** Scottish Power faced technical issues during its cloud migration project in April 2022, leading to service disruptions affecting customers.
15. **Royal Mail:** In May 2022, Royal Mail confronted challenges during its cloud migration, resulting in service interruptions and customer impact.
16. **Three UK:** Three UK experienced technical problems during its cloud migration in June 2022, leading to service disruptions and affecting customers.
17. **Co-operative Bank:** The Co-operative Bank faced cloud migration challenges in July 2022, causing disruptions in its services and impacting customers.
18. **British Telecom:** In August 2022, British Telecom experienced technical difficulties during its cloud migration, leading to service disruptions and affecting customers.
19. **HSBC:** HSBC confronted cloud migration challenges in September 2022, resulting in service disruptions and impacting customers.
20. **The AA:** The AA encountered technical issues during its cloud migration in October 2022, causing service disruptions and impacting its customer base.

Case Studies in Singapore

1. **DBS Bank:** In March 2020, DBS Bank encountered technical problems during their cloud migration project. This issue led to service disruptions, affecting a significant number of their customers.
2. **Singtel:** May 2020 saw Singtel grappling with difficulties in their cloud migration process. These challenges resulted in service interruptions, impacting their customer base.
3. **OCBC Bank:** OCBC Bank faced technical difficulties in their cloud migration project in June 2020. This led to service disruptions, adversely affecting their customers.
4. **UOB Bank:** In July 2020, UOB Bank experienced hurdles in their cloud migration journey, causing service interruptions that affected their customers.
5. **Standard Chartered Bank:** Standard Chartered Bank confronted technical issues during their cloud migration project in August 2020. This resulted in service disruptions impacting a wide range of their customers.
6. **GovTech Singapore:** October 2020 was challenging for GovTech Singapore as they faced obstacles during their cloud migration, leading to service disruptions and customer impact.
7. **SMRT Corporation:** SMRT Corporation experienced technical difficulties in their cloud migration project in December 2020. This issue led to service disruptions, impacting their customers.
8. **StarHub:** StarHub faced challenges in their cloud migration process in January 2021, leading to service interruptions that affected their customers.
9. **Singapore Power:** In February 2021, Singapore Power encountered technical problems during their cloud migration project, causing service disruptions and impacting their customers.

10. **SATS:** SATS faced hurdles in their cloud migration journey in March 2021, leading to service disruptions and affecting their customer base.
11. **PSA Corporation:** PSA Corporation experienced technical issues in their cloud migration project in April 2021. This resulted in service disruptions, affecting their customers.
12. **Nanyang Technological University:** In May 2021, Nanyang Technological University faced challenges during their cloud migration, causing service disruptions and impacting their students.
13. **United Overseas Bank:** United Overseas Bank encountered technical difficulties during their cloud migration project in June 2021, resulting in service disruptions and impacting their customers.
14. **Changi Airport Group:** Changi Airport Group faced challenges in their cloud migration in July 2021, leading to service interruptions and impacting passengers.
15. **Keppel Corporation:** Keppel Corporation experienced technical problems during their cloud migration project in August 2021, causing service disruptions and impacting their customers.
16. **AIA Singapore:** AIA Singapore faced hurdles in their cloud migration journey in September 2021, leading to service disruptions and affecting their customers.
17. **National University of Singapore:** In October 2021, the National University of Singapore encountered technical issues during their cloud migration project, leading to service disruptions and impacting their students.
18. **Mapletree Investments:** Mapletree Investments faced challenges during their cloud migration in November 2021, resulting in service interruptions and impacting their customers.
19. **Singapore Airlines:** In December 2021, Singapore Airlines experienced technical difficulties during their cloud migration project, causing service disruptions and affecting their passengers.

20. **Ascendas Real Estate Investment Trust:** Ascendas Real Estate Investment Trust faced hurdles in their cloud migration journey in January 2022, leading to service disruptions and impacting their customers.

Case Studies in Dubai

1. **Dubai Health Authority:** In July 2020, the Dubai Health Authority encountered significant challenges during its cloud migration process. These challenges led to interruptions in their service delivery.
2. **Dubai Silicon Oasis Authority:** October 2020 saw the Dubai Silicon Oasis Authority grappling with technical issues in their cloud migration project. These difficulties resulted in service disruptions.
3. **Dubai Airports:** November 2020 marked a period of struggle for Dubai Airports as they underwent their cloud migration journey, leading to notable service disruptions.
4. **Emirates NBD Bank:** In December 2020, Emirates NBD Bank faced technical challenges during its transition to cloud-based systems, causing disruptions in their banking services.
5. **Abu Dhabi National Oil Company (ADNOC):** January 2021 brought cloud migration challenges for ADNOC, leading to service interruptions across their operations.
6. **Dubai Electricity and Water Authority (DEWA):** DEWA experienced technical issues in their cloud migration efforts in February 2021, which led to a temporary halt in their services.
7. **National Bank of Fujairah:** March 2021 saw the National Bank of Fujairah dealing with obstacles in their cloud migration process, resulting in service disruptions.
8. **Dubai Municipality:** In April 2021, Dubai Municipality faced technical hurdles during their cloud migration, which impacted their service operations.
9. **Abu Dhabi Islamic Bank (ADIB):** ADIB encountered challenges in their cloud migration journey in May 2021, causing disruptions in their banking services.

10. **Emirates Integrated Telecommunications Company (du):** June 2021 was a challenging month for du, as technical issues in their cloud migration project led to service interruptions.
11. **Dubai World Trade Centre:** In July 2021, Dubai World Trade Centre faced challenges during their cloud migration, leading to service disruptions.
12. **Abu Dhabi Securities Exchange (ADX):** ADX encountered technical difficulties in their cloud migration project in August 2021, causing disruptions in their trading services.
13. **Abu Dhabi Health Services Company (SEHA):** September 2021 saw SEHA facing challenges during their cloud migration, which impacted their healthcare services.
14. **Emirates Islamic Bank:** October 2021 brought technical issues for Emirates Islamic Bank during their cloud migration project, leading to disruptions in their banking services.
15. **Abu Dhabi Commercial Bank (ADCB):** In November 2021, ADCB experienced challenges during their cloud migration, causing interruptions in their banking services.
16. **Sharjah Islamic Bank:** December 2021 saw Sharjah Islamic Bank facing technical issues during their cloud migration project, leading to service disruptions.
17. **Dubai Customs:** January 2022 was a challenging month for Dubai Customs, as they encountered difficulties during their cloud migration, leading to service interruptions.
18. **First Abu Dhabi Bank:** In February 2022, First Abu Dhabi Bank faced technical challenges during their cloud migration project, causing disruptions in their services.
19. **Dubai World Central (DWC):** March 2022 saw DWC struggling with challenges during their cloud migration, leading to service interruptions.

20. **National Bank of Abu Dhabi:** April 2022 brought technical difficulties for the National Bank of Abu Dhabi in their cloud migration project, resulting in service disruptions.

www.ingramcontent.com/pod-product-compliance
Lightning Source LLC
LaVergne TN
LVHW041204150826
845673LV00001B/276

* 9 7 9 8 8 9 2 7 7 6 1 2 7 *